DISOBEDIENT GOD

*DIS*OBEDIENT GOD

Trusting a God Who Goes Off-Script

ALBERT TATE

New York   Nashville

FaithWords
Hachette Book Group
1290 Avenue of the Americas, New York, NY 10104
faithwords.com
twitter.com/faithwords

First Edition: April 2023

FaithWords is a division of Hachette Book Group, Inc. The FaithWords name and logo are trademarks of Hachette Book Group, Inc.

The publisher is not responsible for websites (or their content) that are not owned by the publisher.

The Hachette Speakers Bureau provides a wide range of authors for speaking events. To find out more, go to hachettespeakersbureau.com or email HachetteSpeakers@hbgusa.com.

Unless otherwise noted, all Scripture quotations are taken from the Holy Bible, New International Version®, NIV®. Copyright © 1973, 1978, 1984, 2011 by Biblica, Inc.™ Used by permission of Zondervan. All rights reserved worldwide. www.zondervan.com. The "NIV" and "New International Version" are trademarks registered in the United States Patent and Trademark Office by Biblica, Inc.™

Scripture quotations marked (ESV) are taken from the ESV® Bible (The Holy Bible, English Standard Version®), copyright © 2001 by Crossway, a publishing ministry of Good News Publishers. Used by permission. All rights reserved.

Scripture quotations marked (KJV) are from the Holy Bible, King James Version.

FaithWords books may be purchased in bulk for business, educational, or promotional use. For information, please contact your local bookseller or the Hachette Book Group Special Markets Department at special.markets@hbgusa.com.

Library of Congress Cataloging-in-Publication Data has been applied for.

ISBNs: 9781546000563 (hardcover), 9781546000587 (ebook)

Printed in the United States of America

LSC-C

Printing 1, 2023

This book is dedicated to all of those who've ever wrestled with God and doubted Him, His goodness, and His faithfulness. It's for those who've got more questions than answers. It's for those who've sat in frustration over what God, in His sovereign power, has allowed in their life. It's for those who've watched God go off-script—who've seen Him do things they would never have signed up for. It's for those who've seen God be disobedient in their lives and don't know what comes next.

This is for you. I hope you find and rediscover the goodness, the faithfulness, and the kindness of God—even in His disobedience.

Contents

Foreword

Life's hardest questions seek answers that land on solid ground for the sake of real life now. Questions asked over millennia, philosophical and practical, continue to be asked in part because they matter so much and also because they bring us in touch with mystery; so it is not necessarily easy and fast. Nothing is more profound to consider than whether there is a God, for example, and, if there is, what is God like? If God does exist, and if God is the God made known in Jesus Christ, then this profound good news lands in real time and space: where we all live. But what happens for us when God doesn't act in the ways we might expect? When the satisfaction of knowing God can make us feel lost, disappointed, betrayed by God?

Foreword

Albert Tate lifts up some of these complex questions about life, God, pain, suffering, limitations, doubt, and more—in order to help us get reoriented when God is the one who seems disobedient. That is, when it seems like God is not acting like God, not meeting what we expect or demand God to be. It can feel like God is doing the opposite of what we would imagine. In those really difficult times of disorientation, our lives can feel like they have been turned upside down, leaving us lost or even betrayed. What Albert offers here are pathways to admit these experiences as he is personally honest, passionate, and clear about the times when God has been "disobedient" in his experience and that of others he knows. In his provocative and candid style, Albert turns the spotlight on such "disobedience," and points out many of the ways it seems our crises are about God's disobedience, not ours.

What happens when God is the one who "goes astray" and fails to live out the story line we thought we could expect? We believe God is our protector, until suddenly pain, disease, or tragedy comes our way and it feels like God has gone off-script, disobeyed what we thought God would provide or prevent. We believe God is going to fulfill our dreams, or at least our needs, but we just feel abandoned, damaged, or even destroyed. God's the one who went astray, isn't He? These experiences raise all kinds of questions about God that we need to ask: What? Why? Who? We can find ourselves disoriented about the very thing we felt sure not to fear—until our life experience shocks and confuses us.

What you will find in this book is Albert Tate's personal and pastoral grappling with these real experiences of disappointment and disorientation. He provides windows from his personal story, in season and out of season, when the anguish he names for us is the struggle he has passed through himself. He brings these human realities into practical conversation with the Bible and the Bible's own ways of naming the same things over the long arc of Scripture's narrative.

This is a book of honesty and a book of encouragement. We are not humanly alone with our pains and confusions—others are alongside us. We are not without a God who fails to see and feel and understand our anguish and need—Jesus Christ shares and bears the very struggles we know. In this combination of honesty and God's revelation in Christ, and through the surrounding witness of the Body of Christ, we can "taste and see that the Lord is good," even in bitter and difficult times. God is with and for us in the midst of life's toughest stuff. Albert offers no easy answers. Instead, he bears witness to the freedom of God and the faithfulness of God that explains our hope.

God longs to speak to us in the midst of life's most difficult times. May this honest and clarifying book help us to hear and trust this Word of Life.

Dr. Mark Labberton, Clifford L. Penner
Presidential Chair Emeritus and
Professor Emeritus of Preaching,
Fuller Theological Seminary

Prelude Prayer

Hospitality and Closed Rooms

Sunday morning. As a kid growing up in Pearl, Mississippi, Sunday morning was the culmination of the whole week. Mom would wake us all up early, and immediately we could smell the fresh aroma of food coming from the kitchen. Now, you would think this food aroma was your typical Southern breakfast—smoked sausage, eggs, grits—but actually, no, this wasn't that. We had pot roast, baked chicken, and macaroni and cheese—and this was Sunday dinner. See, my mother has always had the gift of hospitality. When she'd finally get us up, we'd find that she'd already been awake for hours cooking Sunday dinner. By the time

1

we got back from church, the food just needed to be warmed up and it was all ready to go to bring to my grandmother's.

When I tell you Sundays were an experience in our community, I really mean it. Our family would leave our double-wide trailer and drive a few miles up the street to Sweet Home Church of Christ Holiness USA. We'd usually make it to Sunday school and head to our Sunday school classes, and after that, we'd have a brief break. During the break most of the kids would grab snacks, candy, or gum—but what we really wanted to do was sneak and eat during the church service, which started at eleven o'clock. Usually the service would start with a few deacons singing a few hymns, and then they would open up the floor for what we call testimony service. Now, during testimony service, instead of a traditional sermon being preached, we would simply just stand and brag on God's goodness, faithfulness, and sovereignty. We would pass the mic. Different people would stand and share their stories: They talked about how they needed God to move in the doctor's appointment they had coming up on Friday morning at 9:00. They talked about seeing God move and getting a great result from a test. They talked about how they needed a bill paid and they had more month than they had money, but a check came in the mail and it was the exact amount for the bill that needed to be paid. I can remember being a little boy sitting in these services, just being overwhelmed at how good, how faithful, and how kind God was. It was formative to me. We even saw miracles. I remember being in a church service one time and a man who couldn't walk without a cane came to receive prayer and God healed his leg right before our very eyes. They hung his cane on the wall as a testament of God's faithfulness and as the man walked back home healed, it was a celebration like I had never seen before. So, a part of my formative years and my development as a disciple was seeing and hearing the testimonies and the stories of God's consistency, grace, mercy, and favor.

Truly, even our funerals were marked by God's goodness. Some of my earliest memories are going to funerals of great-aunts or great-uncles. We called them homegoing celebrations. They were marked with great exclamation, great celebration, singing, dancing, and of course, tears. We cried and we mourned, but we did it with a hope and a joy that at times was absolutely unspeakable. So, when I think about how I was raised and the role that church played in my upbringing, I see that everything has always been pointing to God's goodness, favor, and timeliness.

When it comes to God's timing, one of the old things we would say is, He may not come when you want it, but He's always, always right on time. I've always carried that with me.

Well, we'd wrap Sunday service up and we'd make it back to our homes and then, *finally*, we would sit and have Sunday dinner. Now, mind you, it was probably around two o'clock in the afternoon, but we called it dinner because by the time we got done eating, resting, and eating again, it would cover lunch and dinner and a late-night snack.

Now, another strong memory growing up was that when we would go to my grandmother's house, there were rooms that you just weren't allowed to go in and there were tables that you just weren't allowed to sit at. At Grandma's the tables were split into two places: the adults' table and the kids' table. So, the kids stayed at their table and the adults ate at their table, which was usually in the nice dining room where the good furniture was sometimes covered in plastic. The kids couldn't go in there and you definitely couldn't take any food in there. The room was absolutely off-limits, but sometimes I'd go and just stand in the doorway and look at it in awe. I would think to myself, "One day when I grow up, I'm gonna go in there and I'm gonna sit down." One time while I was daydreaming, I heard my mother telling me, "Boy, get from over there by that room. You know you ain't got no business going up in there!" There were just rooms that we weren't permitted to go in, even though the house was marked by Grandma's hospitality. Even though it was a time for great celebration, there were rooms and tables that we just didn't go to or sit at. It was a spoken rule that we never broke. Now, as I reflect on what it meant to be discipled and informed by such great joy and celebration and testimonies of God's faithfulness, I see that our faith can be a lot like Grandmother's house on Sunday afternoon—I discovered that there are theological rooms that we just didn't have permission to go in. There were tables of doubt and struggle that we just weren't allowed to sit at.

In church we talked about when God showed up on Tuesday at two o'clock, just like I needed Him. We talked about and would celebrate the times when we needed the doctor's report to come back a certain way and it did. But we never talked about the times when we needed God at two o'clock on Tuesday and He didn't show up. We never expressed the burden and the devastation of needing a bill to be paid and the exact amount not showing up in a check in the mail. When we wanted and needed it, there weren't moments or spaces given to us for wrestling with the reality of disappointment. These were theological rooms that we didn't go into.

These were tables of doubt that we were never invited to sit at. And when you're excluded from these places long enough, it creates a challenge with our faith. It creates this unnecessary hypocrisy, if you will. It creates this unnecessary dichotomy in how we live. We can explain God when He's on time. We can explain God when we know what He's doing. We can explain God when He's matching our prayer request to a T. But how do we talk about God when He doesn't make sense? The moments when we really need Him in a certain time and a certain space, and He doesn't show—how do we make sense of God? How do we deal with these places that we're not allowed to go?

I want to grant us all permission to go to places in our relationship with God where, quite honestly, He doesn't make sense.

I want to extend an invitation to tell the truth about those frustrating moments when He doesn't come when we want Him—when it feels like He's gone off-script and He's doing what He wants to do and not what we want Him to do.

Prelude Prayer

Joy, celebration, and excitement are all great attributes for our relationship with God, but there are more, too: There's grief. There's loss. There's lament. Anger. Fear. Those are all emotional and spiritual postures that shape us throughout the many seasons of our life. But so often it feels like that room's been closed off, that we don't have permission to go there, especially not with God. I'm supposed to have faith, not fear. I'm supposed to have joy, not depression. I'm supposed to have hope, not despair. So when those realities hit us, I fear that we don't have a place. We don't have a table to sit at. We don't have a room to go in. So we're just forced to do one of the worst things we can do in our walk with God, and that's to fake it till we make it. We're thinking, "I guess I just gotta act like I have joy when I'm really struggling with depression. I've gotta act like I have hope when I'm really fighting back despair. I've gotta act like I'm thankful to God for what He's doing when I'm really honestly angry at God for what He's doing or for what He has allowed in His sovereignty."

I think in order for us to really understand who God is, especially in the moments when He goes off-script, we've gotta give permission to go into rooms where grief is allowed, where lament is allowed, where our expression of our frustration and anger and disappointment, even with God, is allowed. In 2020 when the pandemic hit and everything was shut down abruptly, you remember that we all thought we were just going home for two weeks. That turned into two years. And now things are opening back up and life is heading toward a new normal because, let's face it, I don't think it's ever going back to its old normal. But we have this new normal now, and we've been craving it because we're still wading through uncertainty and pain and trauma. The pandemic has been hard on everyone, and we still don't know how devastating the effects have been or will be as time goes on. Personally, what's amazing to me is that I'm still discovering loss. I'm still identifying areas in my life where I'm grieving things that I didn't even realize I lost. For example, my daughter was supposed to start her first year of high school, but she, like so many other people, lost the opportunity to walk across the stage as she transitioned from junior high into her freshman year.

Many people have family members who died, and they lost the opportunity to say goodbye to their loved ones at traditional services. Legacies and traditions were lost. For two full years we lost the ability to see people at church. We actually lost people. There are some people who we haven't seen or heard from. I'm sure they're still alive, but we've just lost the community. We've lost the fellowship. We've lost their presence. And when you have lost so much, you see how underprepared you are to deal with what you haven't practiced well. We haven't practiced getting God's permission to go into the rooms of grief and lament to express that loss. We're so quick to go to joy and happiness and this creates two extremes: Either I'm all the way happy, or I walk all the way away from the faith. Either I walk in complete joy, or I just say, "This must not be for me. Something must be wrong with me." And so we go to what we feel most naturally: depression and discouragement. But this isn't the way because, if you didn't know, living absent of God's purpose and will makes you think and feel the same things—depression and discouragement. We find ourselves either walking fully toward God with a denial of the frustration we feel toward Him, or we walk completely away from God without acknowledging the complexity and the nuance that is following Jesus Christ.

We live in a time where we feel this pressure to say, "Everything's going to be okay." And you know what? That statement is true. I feel in God's sovereign power and His reign, everything will be okay. But today, everything is not okay—and it's okay for everything to not be okay today. It's okay to not be okay.

One of the first messages that I preached during the pandemic was a message on how we get to grieve. We get to cry, we get to be frustrated. We get to sit in loss. We get to look toward heaven with more questions than we have answers. We get to have anger and frustration, even toward God. He's not intimidated by it, but oftentimes we don't give ourselves permission to sit and grieve because we think it's disrespectful or ungrateful. But can I point something out to you? There's a reason why there's a whole book of the Bible called Lamentations.

The book of Lamentations is dedicated to lamenting just these moments. So, I want to give you permission over the next few pages: as we look at a God who is known for His goodness and His greatness and His kindness, we must also understand that He's also known to make some turns that we don't preapprove. He's known for making stops along the journey that we didn't sign off on. He makes calls that we would never make. He invites us to sit in what He would call the beauty of pain while we would see it as the threat of devastation. And in those moments where you find yourself experiencing pain and loss and devastation, I want to give you permission to go into the room of lament and grief, because your pain is worthy and you're allowed to do both.

Your loss is worthy of grief. Your trauma is worthy of time. Acknowledging all that has happened to you and all that you feel is important and necessary, and my encouragement in the pages ahead will be to see how we can invite God into those moments so that we are not left to our own vices.

So how do we invite the God of all creation to sit with us in the dark? How do we do this while acknowledging and recognizing fully that in His sovereignty, He allowed this pain—but that we can't go through it without Him? We need Him if we're going to survive the pain itself.

Now, one last note as we conclude: math ain't faith, and the two don't necessarily go together. What I mean by that is that even after you lament and after you sit in some things that are undone and remain unresolved, it's important to know that it's not a math problem. All the numbers just may not add up. Two plus two may not always be four. Sometimes two plus two is one, sometimes two plus two is two hundred seventy-two. God's economy and God's math don't always equate a full resolve or result in an even number. So, if you're looking for math at the end of this season, if you're looking for one correct answer, if you're looking for one single number, let me tell you now that the power of faith doesn't show up in one single resolved number. It's not about the answer. Oftentimes it's about the journey and it is on the journey that you discover the deep treasures of God's faithfulness and His presence. This is where you find resolve.

When I was a kid, I struggled with math. I mean, if I'm honest, as an adult I still struggle with math. It was *always* a difficult subject for me. I still haven't figured out the algebraic FOIL system with the inside first and the outside or whatever. Honestly, I don't know. When I went to Bible college, the only math class I had to take was the book of Numbers and I passed that with flying colors. But I do remember as a kid thinking that I had found a breakthrough to my mathematical academic challenges. One day my math book fell open to the back of the book. And there I discovered the answers to all the math problems were *in the back of the book*. Can you believe this? Oh my God, I just struck gold! No one ever said anything about this. I'd been struggling trying to get the right answers, and they were all right there!

Prelude Prayer

As you can imagine, my math homework went to another level. I started killing the game. I was getting right answer after right answer and I was turning my math work in and getting great scores. Until finally, my teacher called me and asked me to stay after class. I thought, "Oh, well, this is what happens to high-performing students. This is what happens to kids who get As. The teacher holds them after class to compliment them."

My teacher was named Ms. Jackson. When we met after class, she said to me, "Albert, I've noticed your homework and you're getting better scores, but I'm concerned." I said, "Well, Ms. Jackson, what's the concern?" She said, "I'm seeing your answers, but I'm not seeing your work." So, I said, "Ms. Jackson, what do you mean?" And she said, "Albert, you've got the right answers to the problems, but what I wanna see is the work you did to get those answers. Because what's more valuable to me is not the right answer, but the right work. If you learn how to do the right work, you'll get to the right answers eventually every time. But if you just walk in with the answer and you don't learn how to do the right work, then you miss the joy of the journey of developing and understanding math."

Wow.

You see, oftentimes with God we flood heaven with prayers asking for the right answer and waiting on the right result. We need two, we need six, we need thirty-seven. We need a clear answer. And I believe that God is saying, "You really find joy in the journey. The resolve and peace that you so deeply desire and long for is found not in the right answer, but on the right journey and in the right process of cultivating and developing your faith in My presence along the way."

So as we give permission to lament and to grieve, know that the goal is not to find the right answer. The goal is to faithfully go on the right journey because the journey is marked with God's presence, and eventually, you'll get the right answer every time.

My prayer for you, then, as we begin this journey together, is that we would know the joy and the power and the ways in which we celebrate God's faithfulness, consistency, and goodness in our lives. I pray that we would give ourselves permission to sit at the tables and walk in the rooms of grief and doubt and take time to learn about our God in the midst of pain. Because in these rooms, He is still God. He is still God.

I pray that we would explore His goodness in the midst of bad times and that we would discover His faithfulness in the midst of what feels like inconsistency. I pray that we would find peace in the midst of chaos and that we would be okay with not being okay, trusting that everything's going to be okay. I pray that we'd walk away not with the right answer, but with the right posture to rest and trust in the right God.

Chapter 1

Replace Him

When the people saw that Moses was so long in coming down from the mountain, they gathered around Aaron and said, "Come, make us gods who will go before us. As for this fellow Moses who brought us up out of Egypt, we don't know what has happened to him."

Exodus 32:1

"You took too long!"

Let me start with a few questions. What do we do when something happens that we don't understand? How do we react when we expect God to do one thing, and the complete opposite happens? What do we do when we feel down? And how do we in religious circles react when things aren't good?

Do we talk about the hard times? Do we get angry while we're going through them?

If you're anything like me and most believers I know, our first reaction is to chalk these low moments up to God's sovereignty and completely ignore the pain and the tension of the disappointment we feel.

In other words, we don't let ourselves get angry. We don't let ourselves question God. We don't let ourselves sit in the disappointment of a prayer that seems unanswered, of what feels like an endless season of waiting, of when we ask God for something specific and He does not acquiesce to our request.

But when things are good?

Oh, we're singing *all* the praises. We're sharing our miraculous testimonies with everyone who will listen. We're giving God all the glory and honor for what He's done.

Let me be clear: we *should* be sharing God's compassion and power and divine work in our lives. Testimonies are important. But we can't ignore the hard things or the power of a painful testimony. When we do, we're giving ourselves a false view of who God is and engaging in a limited relationship with Him.

Bottom line: what we need to understand is that our relationship with God may really be more complicated than we realize or are willing to admit.

Sometimes God disappoints us. Sometimes we feel like God's let us down. Sometimes God allows a trial in life so devastating that our whole view of Him is shaken and we can't believe a good God would let such a thing happen.

How do I know this? Because I've been there. Many times. And I'm willing to bet you've been there, too.

Both of my grandfathers were pastors, so from the time I was a small child I grew up in a family of strong faith. In this environment I saw great loss: death, illness, destruction. But I also saw the faith of my family rise. Their faith was so strong and so resilient that it inspired me and strengthened me, and it continues to do so as part of the legacy I received from my parents and grandparents. But, though I have received this great legacy of faith from my family, over time I began to realize I was missing something.

In short, I was benefiting from the fruit of their faith, but I didn't appreciate or really recognize the full scope of it.

Religious circles often have a culture of making sure that God stays in a nice, neat box with a bow. That each of His decisions and moves are understandable. That He *always makes sense.*

From my limited understanding of my family's faith, God always made sense. He always obeyed. Even when things felt bad, they really weren't because God was always good and always made everything better. If you were ever upset with God or confused by Him? You didn't tell Him about it. You just put that feeling away and remembered all the good.

I think we people of faith think this way because we have a need to have our experiences make sense. We want to be able to trace God's moves and decisions and see exactly what He's doing in our lives.

But that isn't the reality of faith or life.

Sometimes God allows a death, an illness, or the loss of a job to disrupt our lives. When that happens, we want to quickly resolve the pain and devastation because we can't handle the reality that God did something we were not okay with. Something we didn't want. Something that hurt.

My grandfathers pastored for over forty years before, during, and after the Civil Rights Movement. They were Black men raising Black families during a time in America where they saw great tragedy, felt great sorrow, and endured great trials that didn't make sense to them. Many Black families can relate. In his book *Bonhoeffer's Black Jesus: Harlem Renaissance Theology and an Ethic of Resistance*, theologian and scholar Reggie L. Williams talks about how faith in God played a major part in the lives and wellness of Black Americans. These people had grandparents and parents who had been slaves. They were living through Jim Crow. They were enduring violence, assault, and racism. They *knew* suffering. Still, they kept a strong faith. How?

When I reflect on all my grandfathers saw and went through, I wonder at the strength of their faith. How even in the midst of the darkest adversity, they remained faithful.

It's a powerful testament, worthy of the likes of Job, who saw more than his fair share of adversity. But the whole time I was admiring their faith and enjoying this legacy I've received as my inheritance, I was missing something. My family has a strong faith foundation—that's true. But I wasn't seeing the whole picture.

Ultimately, I was missing the *labor* of their faith. I was unaware of the rejection they felt, the doubt, the struggle to believe, and the deep suffering that shaped and strengthened their belief. In doing so, I had created a God who was inundated with His goodness and faithfulness, but one with whom I didn't know how to sit in suffering and rejection.

My grandfathers knew how to do this with great joy. They knew how to doubt and question and struggle, and because of this their faith was strong.

We as a society have lost this ability to see both God's faithfulness and His rejections. To us, the two cannot coexist. We don't know how to sit in pain and anger and invite God in. We want to move past the discomfort and hurt feelings and wait for His blessings to rain down again. But a faith where you expect God to cosign on all your life plans on your timeline and at your demand is a shallow faith.

We tend to treat our relationship with God like this: so long as we do everything right, God will make everything in our lives go right. When that doesn't happen, we're suddenly at a loss and God has become disobedient to our desires and what we think should (and should not) happen.

This faith is weak because it misses the reality of life and the fullness of who God is, what He can do, and what He *wants* to do in your life. The minute hardship comes, this kind of faith falls apart and you miss God altogether.

If I had to sum all of this up in one sentence, it would be this: **strong faith comes from deep rejection, painful losses, doubt, discomfort, and suffering.**

There are no shortcuts to developing strong faith. This means that walking with Jesus doesn't erase the painful moments of life. In fact, walking with Jesus means that rejection and suffering are sure to come. But it is these exact seasons that strengthen your faith. It is in these moments that you see God most clearly.

Not exactly what you wanted to hear? Me neither. These are hard words to swallow and our flesh immediately wants to reject them. But they're important, and we're just getting started.

Now, let's take a look at Exodus.

There's a very interesting picture found in the book of Exodus, around chapter 32. An encounter happens in that passage of Scripture that completely shapes the conversation I want to have with you.

Let's set the scene: It's the children of Israel. They've been delivered out of Egypt. They've seen God's hand of faithfulness: He came in, He set them free, He brought them out. Now Moses is up on the mountain with God, and we later find out that He's giving Moses the vision of how to love Him through the Ten Commandments. It's a vision Moses is to give the children of Israel.

But the people aren't up on the mountain with Moses. They're waiting...and they're waiting. They've come out of Egypt, and they've passed through the Red Sea that God parted for them. God has spared them, but now they're just waiting. And in their waiting they grow frustrated and weary, to the point where they look at Moses' brother and right-hand man, Aaron, and say, "Aaron, God is taking too long. He's not following our timeline. He's not moving according to the schedule that we anticipated. God is not following our instructions. God is way off-script. *God is being disobedient.*"

So, they tell Aaron to build a calf. *We need another god* is essentially the message.

They replace their God—*the* God—with the golden calf. Where does this golden calf come from? It comes from Egypt, this familiar place from their past where they had seen idol worship. They had seen these gods erected, and they had seen these gods worshipped. So instead of trusting their God who had brought them out of Egypt, instead of trusting their God who had brought them through the Red Sea, instead of trusting their God who had drowned and destroyed their enemies, in that first moment of crisis when God went off-script and didn't do what they thought He ought to do, they went *back*.

When God was disobedient, then they immediately reverted to what was familiar instead of trusting Him who had been faithful. They went back to their Egyptian ways; they built a god made of gold. They built a god they could push around. They built a god they could control, who would do what was expected of him. A god who would stay on-script and *obey*.

Aaron looked at the people and said, "Give me your gold." After seeing what the people did when God didn't obey them, he decided to do what they asked instead of reminding them what they really needed.

Isn't it interesting how they were reaching for gold, and yet really longing for God? Which raises the question: **What are you reaching for and what are you longing for, and do you know the difference?**

When God Goes Off-Script in Your Life

We serve a God who doesn't always follow our instructions—I mean, prayer requests.

He has a way of doing His own thing. He adds twists and turns. He adds highs and lows. He adds dimensions and dynamics to your story, a texture that you *never* would have approved. He allows storms and crises to show up that you would never cosign. In fact, you wouldn't even think about allowing that circumstance to show up in your family—but here it is. So, what do you do?

Have there been seasons or times in your life when God just took too long? You had a deadline, you had a time frame, you had a place when you needed Him to show up. Maybe it was when you needed cancer to be healed, maybe it was when you had a bill that needed to be paid, maybe it was when you wanted to be in a relationship, you wanted to be married, and you set a deadline. Maybe it was when you wanted to be pregnant by a certain time, and God just didn't show up.

Let's be honest about those seasons and those moments. The question that I'm asking you is *What was your response?*

What do you do when God takes too long? What do you do when He begins to write the script of your story that you have not approved or envisioned?

Your Golden Calves

Let's talk about the golden calf. When God was disobedient, the people of Israel said, "Let's replace Him."

So many times, we reach for things that are simply cheap counterfeits of the real thing. They were longing for God, but they reached for gold. We do the same thing.

Replace Him

Got any golden calves lying around the house? Got any golden calves at the office? Got any golden-calf relationships that you fall back to?

When the crisis comes or when God takes too long, oftentimes we replace Him—and what we grab is the nearest golden calf we can find, the most recent thing from Egypt. Egypt represents sin, and Satan wants you to go back to pleasing yourself. He wants you to reach for control. He wants you to walk by what's familiar and not walk by faith. He wants you to be annoyed and put off by God's disobedience.

On the other hand, God knows that in order for you to truly follow Him, "you've got to trust His heart when you cannot trace His hand," as someone once said.

But the first time the journey gets rough, the first time things get a little rocky, you immediately grab not God, not faith, but what's familiar.

You're walking in security and depending on God and you've got yourself together . . . and then comes that first low day. You text who's familiar instead of praying to Who's been faithful. As soon as you hit rock bottom, you grab the bottle that's familiar instead of drinking the Living Water that's been faithful.

Where's your golden calf? Where do you hide it? Most of us don't keep it in plain sight—we stick it away.

But as soon as things get rough, we say, "Aw man, let me go get this calf because I can push it around, I can control it, I can dictate where it goes. It doesn't surprise or disappoint me. *It obeys me.*"

What's your golden calf? What's your go-to? Maybe it's a hamburger, maybe it's pizza, maybe it's the nearest buffet. As soon as God does something that you didn't plan or schedule or expect, you immediately react by feasting on food instead of feasting on the faithfulness of God. Maybe you find the god of alcohol so you can numb the pain and you worship at the altar of intoxication. You find the god of money so that you can make some attempt at having power and influence, thinking now you have control—and you worship at the altar of your own control, influence, and power.

When God doesn't show up when you want Him to, what do you replace Him with?

Golden Calf Sighting: The Hidden Addiction

I looked at my wife, LaRosa, and she looked at me. We really didn't know what to say next because sitting in between us was this huge golden calf—and there was no way to talk around it. It was no longer hidden, and for the first time in our marriage we were forced to deal with this golden calf.

We'd gotten to that moment because we were watching *Oprah* (don't judge me, I'm a huge *Oprah* fan. I would watch the show all the time if I could). This was our newlywed season of life, no kids, and she and I were just relaxing, sitting on our bed watching *Oprah* in our little seven-hundred-square-foot apartment, our first home in Southern California.

Kirk Franklin was her guest on this episode, and LaRosa and I are huge gospel music fans, so he and Oprah coming together was an epic moment for us. Then something happened that we didn't expect: Kirk began to talk about an addiction he had. Now, this is a big deal because he's a Christian recording artist on the biggest platform in the world, *The Oprah Winfrey Show*—and he's talking about...addiction? Kirk Franklin talked about his childhood, he talked about sexuality and struggles, and then he talked about his addiction to pornography.

Slowly, I began to sink into the bed. His honesty, his transparency, his vulnerability were causing me to literally shrink. I could not hide small enough as he told about his struggle with pornography, his lies to his wife, his deceit, his desire to quit but then how he'd go back to it. He shared a vivid story of taking videotapes and throwing them in the dumpster, but the addiction had such control in his life that he went back, dug in the dumpster, and got the tapes out so that he could continue to watch them.

My wife and I sat there and watched him telling his story in stunned disbelief. I don't remember even talking during the commercials. We sat there transfixed at the words that were coming out of his mouth: the story of his addiction; the story of how he and his wife worked through the crushing brokenness and overcame it. Oprah, with her amazing interviewing ability, brought out the raw, honest pain and power of a pornography addiction.

The show ended, the audience applauded, and then—I'll never forget it—my wife turned and looked at me and said, "Do you struggle with pornography?" There was a long pause and in that silent moment, I knew I couldn't hide it anymore. "Yes," I said. And that's when the golden calf was exposed. I couldn't cover it up. It was out, and we had to do something about it.

When I was a little boy, I was exposed to pornography.

Back then it was magazines and VHS tapes; as technology evolved, so did my addiction. As a single pastor struggling, I remember thinking, "When I get married, this addiction will be healed." The irony is, I was a minister of the gospel and never once considered that Jesus could heal my pornography addiction then. You know the fallacy of the lie that I was telling myself— marriage did not heal or cure or deliver me from my addiction to pornography. Marriage only exposed pornography for the deceitful lie that it is. Pornography has nothing to do with real, actual sex and intimacy with your spouse.

So, I found myself navigating this addiction that lived in secrecy. I'd given my life to Jesus, was a passionate lover of God, and He was using me. I had a calling on my life, but when it came to sex and intimacy and connection and my singleness, I struggled with God's timing. It was like I was saying, "God, I won't have sex, but I'll just masturbate with pornography. That seems like a nice compromise since You feel like I should wait until I'm married."

I had a problem with God's timing. He was not following the sequence that I would prefer, and that didn't change after marriage. Even then, He was so . . .

disappointing. He did not do what I wanted Him to do. I wanted Him to use my marriage to heal me of any desire, any proclivity to look at pornography. Why would I want to, once I could have all the sex I wanted? (Yes, I hear you laughing at that notion.)

God didn't give me what I wanted. In my passion, my pursuits, my lustful desires—God was disobedient. He did not follow the proclivities of my flesh. So, I found myself in a crisis. My body was yearning for something that I felt I needed to resolve. What I didn't understand was that there is a longing and a passionate desire for intimacy and connection. When I was sitting down at that computer, it wasn't that I just wanted physical sexual pleasure—there was something bigger, deeper happening within me. I was desiring connection; I was desiring to be seen; I was desiring intimacy. In the truest sense, I was desiring God. There I was: longing for intimacy but reaching for pornography. Longing for the intimacy that comes from my God, but instead saying, "Give me the gold."

I grabbed for pornography, creating a golden calf where I bowed and I worshipped because I could pick the timing. I could set it up, I could click on the mouse, and I could get that god to obey whenever I needed it to. With Jesus I'd have to wait. With Jesus I'd have to sacrifice. With Jesus I'd have to not pursue my pleasure and instead pursue His promise and His plan for my life, which didn't always unfold in a microwavable moment whenever I felt like it.

I carried that golden calf around and whenever Jesus was late, whenever I felt lonely, isolated, unseen, insecure, instead of reaching for the one I was longing for, I brought godlike expectations to pornography... and it drastically disappointed me time and again. There wasn't one time when I looked at something on a computer and felt like, "Ahhh, I'm better now." My flesh felt relieved for a moment, but my soul always felt worse. That's the nature of sin: brief relief to your flesh, deep discouragement to your soul, because idols never satisfy—only God does.

Back to that day watching Kirk and Oprah with LaRosa. There I was in our bedroom, looking at my wife and this idol, this golden calf that I'd been carrying, which was now fully exposed. I didn't know how to navigate it.

We had our work cut out for us because unfortunately, I thought that golden calves could stay hidden, but it turns out they can't.

Made to Worship

We are made to worship; we're designed to worship. It's natural. Our hearts long to worship something, and we will bow at the altar of just about anything if in the moment it makes us feel better.

We're so averse to crisis, so averse to discomfort, so averse to disruption that as soon as the disruption comes, we immediately start grabbing familiar comforts as quickly as we can. But God did not call us to comfort. He called us to the kingdom, and that requires a sense of faithfulness and trust when He disrupts us, when He goes off-course, when He goes off-script.

Oftentimes, though, we reject His call and try to find a new god as soon as possible. *I need another god that I can push around. I need another god that I can control. I need something that is going to make me feel better—so let me eat as much as I can, let me drink as much as I can, let me sleep with as many people as I can, let me look at as much pornography as I can. I just need to reach for something because what I am longing for seems so distant. I need to reach for something that appears to be much nearer.*

What are you *reaching* for? And what are you *longing* for behind that reaching? And do you know the difference?

When Golden Calves Come Crashing Down

Back when we lived in Mississippi, my wife and I had the joy of doing ministry together in the youth group at our church. This was before we had children ourselves, so we poured into the youth group kids and they were the loves of our lives. We would do life together: we'd watch movies together; we'd go to camp together; we'd pray together; we'd sing together; and inevitably we'd spend a lot of time eating, laughing, and, yes, crying together.

Lisa was one of our students I'll never forget. She had graduated from high school, gone off to college, and was out having a great career. One day she called and said she was in town and wanted to see us. She wanted to come by for dinner, and these are the moments that you live for as a youth pastor. With current students, you just don't know if they're listening. Maybe they're not paying attention to you; you're wondering if you still got it, if you're still relevant, if this is making a difference in anybody's life. You worry they're all going to hell. So, you look forward to these dinners with past students because you're thinking, "Wow, I've got a success story coming back. I can't wait to hear how she's doing so I can feel better about myself."

That night, Lisa rang the doorbell and there she stood, glowing with success. As we shared a meal together, I thought about how when she was young, her dad passed away, and it was so cool to see the church rally around her in those hard moments of her journey. It was one of those stories where you just saw God do some redemptive things.

We were sitting at the kitchen table, finished with our meal, Mississippi sweet tea sitting in the center of the table, and no need for dessert because there was enough sugar in the tea to satisfy all of our sweet tooths. That's when Lisa's countenance changed and she shifted the conversation. It was no longer about all the successes. I could tell she had come to talk to her youth pastors because she wanted to confess some of her failures.

She began to tell one of the most horrific stories I'd ever heard, how she was date-raped by several men. She woke up in an apartment, exposed, and it was clear in many ways that she'd been violated. But this violation went deep into her mind, her soul—far beyond her body. As she told us this, with tears streaming down her face, she began to confess an extremely promiscuous lifestyle. She told us about how she went from one relationship to another and found herself sleeping with men to comfort herself, meeting men in bars and having these sexual relationships over and over again. "Maybe I have an addiction," she said. "I don't know, I just know that I feel terrible and I don't know what to do—the shame and guilt are overcoming me."

Even while she was telling us that, I could see shame shading her skin. I noticed that she kept referencing the number of men she'd slept with, but she never said the exact number. After a while, it was clear that she had a number, and that number was holding a gun to her head, daring her to say it out loud. This number had taken residence in her mind so that she was shaped by it. This number had become the defining factor in her life, and it was holding her hostage to her past.

As Lisa was telling story after story of loss and rejection and violation and abuse, and the insecurity that she carried, I looked over at my wife and she looked at me as if we both could see clearly what needed to happen next.

I looked at that dear student of ours and said, *"Lisa, tell me the number."* Fear filled her eyes. I could see the despair and the shame. "I can't," she said, and began to talk about all the things we would think about her if we only knew the full story. It was as if the number was saying, "You can't say me out loud because no one will love you after I am made known. No one will see you, no one will respect you. Those success stories you just told at the dinner table will all evaporate; they will be meaningless because this number erases everything."

Still, I just said, *"Tell me the number."* The weight of that number was like Mount Everest sitting on her tongue. She couldn't lift it. But she came to our house for something, and it was as if she didn't want to leave without it. So, in a moment of courage and bravery with her head hung down, not making eye contact at all, she lifted Mount Everest. She opened her mouth, and she said the number.

I didn't even pay attention. I don't even remember what the number was because without hesitation I looked at her and said, *"Lift your head, look at me."* I told her that number doesn't matter. "Here's the number that I need you to know," I said. "3 ... 1 ... 6 ... *For God so loved the world that He gave His only begotten Son that whosoever would believe in Him would not perish but have everlasting life. That number is the only number that gets to define your life."*

Immediately the gun dropped from her head. Grace flooded her soul, and she fell into my wife's embrace. They held each other and cried, those tears washing away the stains of the sin she had been carrying.

Replace Him

Lisa was longing for the love of a Father, but she reached for the lust of men. She did that instead of taking her broken heart, the broken heart of a little girl who lost her daddy way too soon, to her Heavenly Father. I imagine she was probably angry with Him, frustrated, because what God takes a little girl's dad? God was disobedient and went off-script in a way she never would have approved. She was longing for what only He could provide, but she couldn't reach for Him because she was so angry at what He'd done. She ended up reaching for the golden calf of other men's approval when she really longed for her Heavenly Father's care.

When that gun dropped from her head, it was like there was a crashing sound, like metal hitting concrete floors in an industrial building. That crashing sound was the breaking of the golden calf. It echoed deeply in her soul, in our souls, as we were all reminded that although the golden calf is big, although the golden calf can start to define you, to hold you hostage, *the golden calf can be destroyed.* Actually, Tim Keller says, "Idols aren't destroyed, they're replaced." I'd say this one had to be destroyed *and* replaced because that number had to crash; it had to crumble, and we had to replace it with a new number.

This moment was especially pivotal because Lisa

was at the age and stage when many people fall away from their faith journey. They no longer have the faith we have as children (either literally or in the infancy of our relationship with Christ): that God is good and only does good and everything is always good and that's that. They suddenly have room for questions, for doubts, for anger. But instead of bringing these things to God, they walk away.

Suffering begets these questions, these doubts. When suffering comes, we're in danger of falling away because what happened was so traumatic and so devastating that we no longer trust God. How could He have let that happen? How could He have allowed that experience to come to pass? How can He really be good if something so detrimental happened on His watch?

These are big questions, and God wants us to bring them to Him rather than turning to what's immediately comforting and familiar—our golden calves.

Golden calves crumble. They do crash. They may seem invincible, but they can be destroyed. Don't allow them to hold you hostage and keep you stuck in a place where you were never created to be. Maybe it's the number of your income; maybe it's the number that shows up on the scale; maybe it's the number one because you're single and you're not in a relationship.

40

Don't allow any number of this world to define you. Allow the number of the grace of God to define you.

The purpose of this book is to help you understand how you respond when God is disobedient—when He doesn't follow your instructions. It's to help you see that the great tragedy of God's disobedience is not that He went off-script; it's our response. When we reach for golden calves, for substitutes, we suddenly have the power to cause great damage in our lives because in the long run these substitutes don't satisfy—they kill.

Over the following pages I hope that you will better understand the proclivities of your heart, where you tend to wander, where you tend to drift, so that you will know exactly the places where you need to be found.

Chapter 2

Run from Him

I was sitting on the couch in my therapist's office this week unpacking a current challenge I've been struggling with. While I was talking, I summed up my feelings with these words: disappointment, isolation, insecurity, and loneliness. As he listened to me describe this problem I've honestly been overwhelmed by, he proceeded to do the ever-so-popular therapist move that, if it's not your own therapy session, you can usually see coming from a mile away: He asked, "When was the first time you felt this way?" Then he went on: "Do you remember the first time in your childhood when you felt isolated or disappointed or alone or insecure? Take me back there, Albert. Talk about what that time was like."

I thought to myself, "He got me because we all know everything that we're experiencing now comes from something that we've experienced before." In other words, he was on to something. But don't you just hate it when that happens because you know you now have to go back and work that thing out and make it match where you are today? It's good—it's healing even—but it just makes life that much more complicated.

So, I talked about one of my earliest experiences of feeling disappointed: the first time I was bullied as a kid.

I was in sixth grade and people were calling me names. Back then, I was the kid who got on the bus and was immediately met with a joke. Someone would crack a joke about me in the back of the bus and the entire bus would just laugh and laugh. I didn't even know my nose was big until someone announced it on the bus and everyone else started laughing. Tangentially, I think I've grown into it now, for the most part anyway, but I just remember feeling so insecure and embarrassed. To make things worse, mine was one of the last stops on the bus, so I was one of the last to get picked up. So, when I'd get on there and try to find a seat, each one was already filled. Kids were already comfortably grouped together on those two-person benches and here I come needing to be a third. Nobody liked that. No one wanted to sit three to a school bus bench. So each day I would board the bus, endure a joke, and then look desperately around for just one face that was receptive, some eyes that weren't avoiding making contact or looking annoyed, someone who was nice enough to scoot over so I could have a seat. It was honestly a social crisis. Every time I stepped on that bus that first year of middle school was brutal. I was so disappointed in my middle school experience. I felt all alone. And soon my method for coping with all of this was to just...not cope at all. Some people say when a crisis comes, we have a fight-or-flight response. Well, I had no response. I just didn't deal with it. I took flight emotionally and just acted like it didn't happen.

When I would come home from school after a day of isolation, insecurity, and embarrassment and my folks would ask me, "How was your day?" I'd only ever say "Fine" back to them. I honestly think about this when my kids come home and I ask 'em how their day went, and they just say "Fine." It makes me wonder because my "fine" was a lie.

So, it was there in sixth grade that my insecurity was born. When I finished my story, my therapist looked at me and said, "Albert, that's how you learned to deal with things. You ignore them, you isolate, and you tend not to cope with issues. You tend to just push 'em down."

When he said that, I thought to myself, "Wow. I've been acting like that sixth grader all this time—even now as a forty-four-year-old."

This insight was honestly so helpful. My therapist didn't shame me for thinking in an unhealthy way as a forty-four-year-old man. Instead, he equipped me with tools to appreciate and empathize with that sixth grader who just didn't know how to deal with pain and struggle. He showed me how to stop and pay attention to my response when things get hard: How am I reacting? And the bigger question: *Why* am I reacting this way?

This chapter is all about digging deep in your response and understanding why you respond the way you do. More specifically, I'm talking to the people who tend to do like I do: who don't stick around and fight and only take flight emotionally—those of us who run.

Now, when I say the names Jesse Owens, Florence Griffith Joyner, Carl Lewis, or Usain Bolt, you can't help but think of some of the world's greatest runners of all time. And while this is a pretty stacked list, there is one significant runner missing from it. He is one of the most famous runners in the history of humanity. I'm talking about one of the greatest runners in all of Scripture: Jonah.

Jonah was a prophet of the Lord. A prophet is a person whose calling is to deliver words from the Lord to the people they are intended for. Jonah's story as a prophet is told in the Old Testament. It begins with an invitation in chapter 1, verses 1–2: "The word of the LORD came to Jonah son of Amittai: 'Go to the great city of Nineveh and preach against it, because its wickedness has come up before me.'" And that's when we see it: Jonah hears the Lord, but he runs. Like, the man took *off*.

Now, there are several things in his flight to pay attention to:

As we look at the story of Jonah, this world-famous runner, we see that he knew God and God knew him. They had a relationship, and they were obviously familiar with each other. I say this because there are times when we might even question if Jonah actually knew God to begin with, given his behavior, but it was clear: he could hear God's voice.

Do you know how many of us have spent so many hours praying and asking God to please speak? We tell

Him, "I want to hear Your voice. I want to know what my purpose is. I want to know what I'm supposed to do. I want to know how You want to use me. What is my destiny? Speak to me, oh Lord. Speak to me."

We spend hours—years even—journaling, writing, praying, and asking God to speak. And here, Jonah gets just that. God speaks to him. God gives him instruction. God gives him an assignment and it's crystal clear. He knows exactly what it is that he's supposed to do. But immediately after hearing God's voice, Jonah runs.

Obviously, he had a different expectation.

It's apparent that Jonah was willing to hear God, but was he willing to be used by God? Because it's obvious Jonah just wasn't expecting the assignment God gave him. Jonah probably had his own idea of where he wanted to go, what he wanted to do, and to whom he wanted to speak. But God's plans did not fall in line with what Jonah had asked and—dare I say—instructed God to do in his life through his prayer requests.

When I look at prayer requests in the Bible, I often refer to them as *instructions for God* rather than actual prayers. These prayers aren't petitions before God— they're instructions to God, telling Him what we want and expect. We all do this. That's why it's so devastating when God goes off-script—we know He knows what we want Him to do . . . and now He's ignored that. With Jonah, God just goes all the way off-script. He does His own thing. He does not obey any of Jonah's instructions.

We see God, then, through Jonah's eyes: as disobedient. God has not done what Jonah was expecting, and Jonah's not happy with what he's facing. So what does he do to this God who's shown up disobediently in his life? Who's refused to follow his instruction and who has gone off-script? He runs from Him.

Now, I hope that as we look at the life of Jonah, we aren't too harsh. I hope we can see in our own lives the same potential to grab our track shoes and just start running so we can do our own thing. Jonah is not special in this way—in many ways, he's just like you and he's just like me.

So, what do you do with the disobedient God? If Jonah were here, he'd say, "I ran from Him."

Running to a Place That Does Not Exist

Jonah receives his instruction from God and he runs. Verse 3 says that "Jonah ran away from the Lord and headed for Tarshish. He went down to Joppa where he found a ship bound for that port. After paying the fare, he went aboard and sailed for Tarshish to flee from the Lord."

Historians theorize that Joppa and Tarshish were actual places. I don't know if they are. But if you look at the text, it's clear that Jonah is not going to Tarshish as his ultimate destination. His ultimate destination is simply away from the Lord. It's away from God's presence. He is fleeing from the Lord, but Jonah will soon discover that he's running to a place that does not exist.

So, a warning if you are running from God's purpose, God's plan, God's view, God's reign, and God's authority. If you're trying to run from God, you are running to a place that does not exist. It is a futile retreat. And can I tell you? It is not worthy of all the energy, pain, and disruption it will cause in your life. There is no place to run where He isn't there. You won't find it. In Psalm 139:8, David said, "If I go up to the heavens, you are there; if I make my bed in the depths, you are there." David is talking in this beautiful way about how we cannot escape God, and I just really appreciate it because he's not complaining—he's honoring the presence of God.

And yet . . . here's Jonah. Jonah, who is saying, "Man, I'm trying to run from the presence of God." And he doesn't know or understand yet that this place does not exist. If you're a runner, I encourage you to learn from Jonah before you waste a lot of time and effort to go a long way to nowhere.

One of the biggest lessons you'll learn when God goes off-script is that when He doesn't obey your instructions and when you experience and encounter the disobedience of God in your life, you *don't run from it*. I cannot emphasize enough that you cannot outrun the presence of God. You cannot outrun the reign of God. So why start that pointless journey?

Another thing I notice in this passage is that when Jonah leaves for Tarshish, it says he pays a fare for this trip. Let me say that again: Jonah pays a fare to run to a place that does not exist. In other words, his flight cost him something and gained him nothing.

When you decide to live according to your own will, and when you decide to see God's assignment, hear God's voice, and say, "Nah, I'm gonna go somewhere else," well, it's probably gonna cost you more than you were willing to pay.

That's what sin does: it makes you go further than you plan to go, stay longer than you plan to stay, and pay more than you can afford to pay. And when sin is finished with you, it leaves you for dead.

If you're going your own way and if you're running

away from the presence, the power, the purpose, and the plan of God for your life, are you willing to pay that fare? Are you willing to pay what it costs to be your own god and your own boss? Are you willing to pay what it costs to run?

Well, Jonah paid his fare. He got on the ship, and they started going in the opposite direction of God's plan. And then a storm comes. A literal storm. It begins to rage on the ship. It gets so bad that the other people on the ship start praying and casting lots to the gods. It may seem odd that they're doing this, but the truth is that they recognize this storm is not normal. This is not just nature; this is God being angry. And although they believe in the multiplicity of gods, they are trying to cast lots and see which person made their gods angry. Meanwhile, Jonah is asleep on the ship during the storm, and they have to wake him up. The captain goes down below deck where Jonah is sleeping and he says, "How can you sleep at a time like this?"

What a great question.

Jonah was running away from God and now he was asleep. Just completely checked out. How can that be? And does it sound at all familiar? One of the most dangerous things is to sleep at a time like this—to check out at a time like this. To disengage and go numb at a time like this. One of Satan's greatest strategies is to get us to disconnect and go to sleep on the purpose and the plan that God has for our life. And you gotta hear the voice of the Holy Spirit saying, "Wake up! How can you sleep at a time like this?"

Now's not the time to disengage with God. Now's not the time to run away from Him. And it's definitely not the time to go to sleep and ignore the realities of what's happening in your world. What does it mean for you to wake up and engage a God who hasn't given up on you? A God who refuses to allow you to run in the wrong direction?

So, back to Jonah's story: the other men on the ship cast lots to see whose god is angry and the lots fall on Jonah. And Jonah, to his credit, admits this storm is his fault. Then the men say, "Who are you? Who is your God?" And in chapter 1, verse 9 Jonah says, "I am a Hebrew and I worship the LORD, the God of heaven, who made the sea and the dry land." You know what this tells me? It tells me that Jonah didn't just know God, he *knew* who God was. He knew His authority, power, and reign. Which makes me want to ask Jonah, *How?*

How are you going to run away from this God? He made the sea. He made the land. There's no place to go where God's fingerprints aren't already there. Jonah was well aware of the bigness of his God, but he refused to trust and rest in it.

Well, as the storm raged on, it got more violent. The ship was threatening to break apart. The men beg and they ask, "What do we need to do? What do we need to do?" And in verse 12 Jonah says, "Pick me up and throw me into the sea . . . and it will become calm."

It appears that this is a very noble action for Jonah. It almost seems like he's trying to save their lives. But the men don't immediately give up. Unfortunately in Jonah's mind, the only way this could end was for him to be thrown overboard. So inevitably the other passengers throw Jonah overboard.

Though this seems noble, you have to understand that Jonah's not seeking to save their lives—he's seeking to destroy his own. This is the moment where, because of his arrogance, his commitment to not follow God, and his fierce resolve to go his own way, Jonah is saying with his actions that he'd rather die than go to Nineveh and preach. He'd rather end it all than do what God has asked him to do. We have to notice the arrogance of his statement and his directions to the men. He says, "Pick me up and throw me into the sea and it will become calm." Clearly, he still thinks he has control. He still thinks that if he ends it—not if he does what God asks, but if he ends it—then that'll calm everything down and everything will be fine.

So, he goes into the sea thinking that he's ending something, but the reality is that something is just now beginning.

Jonah gives up. He quits. He throws in the towel with a final act of control. He tries to end it all as he goes into the sea and in that moment he gives up on God—but God doesn't give up on him. Jonah had his pen, he was writing his story, and he wrote the end of his story. He put a period at the end of the sea. But his period gets interrupted by grace and quickly becomes a comma thanks to . . . a great fish.

The text says the Lord provides a fish to swallow Jonah, which, ultimately, saves him from a watery grave. And he spends three days and nights in the belly of this fish, sometimes called the leviathan.

Now, with such an ending to chapter 1, it's probably no surprise to anyone that chapter 2 begins with a prayer. From within the belly of the fish, Jonah begins praying to the Lord his God, asking Him to save him from this situation that, as we clearly see, Jonah got himself into.

I know it's getting good, but let me pause a moment

and tell you about my best friend, Ricky Jenkins. I promise it's going to connect.

Now, when we were young men, my friend Ricky would always run out of gas. He had this brand-new red 1995 Camaro that he was so proud of. But I'm telling you, without fail, when we would drive down the streets of Pearl, Mississippi, Ricky would always run out of gas. It became common to see that red Camaro parked on the side of the road and Ricky walking to the nearest gas station, only to return with a full gas can in hand. Everyone saw him, but nobody was ever trying to pick him up. Nobody was ever helping. They just saw Ricky go by and knew what was up. You might be wondering why Ricky didn't just keep his tank filled. I don't know the reason, but I do know Ricky loved living on the edge. He loved seeing how far he could get that Camaro to go when it was on E. And so he would ride that thing out, and he would inevitably run out of gas.

One day Ricky and I were at a church conference. I walked outside at one point and saw this very disturbing scene: Ricky is literally in a physical tussle with a friend of ours named Sam. It was so odd because Sam and Ricky are wrestling and they're fighting *in the street*, but we aren't kids. To see Ricky fighting someone at all is just not normal…even more so in this situation. We are all grown men, and we're in *ministry* at a *church conference*. Not really the place for a brawl. I'm so taken aback I immediately jump in and try to break them up. Then, I see Ricky gesturing to the ground as he continues to battle Sam. So I look and I see there's this pill bottle. I look back at Ricky and now he's pointing back to Sam and I put two and two together.

Sam had taken a bottle of pills in a suicide attempt, and Ricky was trying to force Sam into the Camaro so he could get him to the hospital. I joined forces with Ricky and I grabbed Sam. We overpowered him and shoved him in the back seat of the red Camaro, and when we were ready to go, Ricky took off—he just punched it to the Rankin General Hospital. We're flying down the streets and while we're in the car, Sam isn't saying anything. His eyes are bloodshot, he's crying, and he looks so angry. He just looks furious. While he's not saying anything, Ricky and I are peppering him with questions: *What were you doing? What are you thinking? What's wrong? Are you okay? What's going on? Why did you do this?* And Sam's just not answering.

Finally, we pull up to the emergency room. We jump out. We start pulling Sam out of the back seat of the car, and we're both trying to force him into the

emergency room. Some attendants notice us all struggling, so they come help and bring a wheelchair. We get
Sam down in the wheelchair and I swear it's almost like
a scene from a movie: we're rolling in and the medics
are bombarding us with the same questions we were
asking Sam: *What's wrong? What happened?* We're telling them that we found him trying to overdose on some
pills. And in the midst of all the questions, they asked,
"Well, what pills did he take?" And Ricky and I just
shout out the name of pills we thought he took.

Well, after hearing our description of the pill, the
nurse immediately says he can't die from that. In fact,
she makes it clear that there's not even a chance Sam
will be sick after taking the pills he did, let alone in
danger of dying.

Sam's face immediately falls. He was clearly so dis-
gusted by the news from the nurse that I could almost
see what he was thinking: "Yet another failure. I can't
even do this right." And in the next moment he jumps
up out of the chair and walks back outside. Ricky and
I follow him, and some of the nurses follow us, asking
if there's anything they can do to help. Neither of us
knew what to say, so we said no.

Now, the three of us were all sitting outside. Sam is
there, sitting alone, obviously wrestling with issues way

beyond anything that he felt comfortable explaining to us. And now he's dealing with this new reality, this new failure, and I'm sure he's feeling embarrassed, angry, disappointed, and just so, so sad.

So, Ricky and I are sitting there not really knowing what to do. Finally we figure, let's just go back to the conference. I mean, there's no point in us sitting in the parking lot of this hospital emergency room anymore.

So, Sam loads into the back seat, Ricky and I load into the front, and still all this time Sam hasn't said a word. Tears are streaming down his face. His eyes are still bloodshot, and we've given up on trying to get him to talk.

We're about to drive back to the conference, but before we can get out of the parking lot and out onto the street, Ricky's car runs out of gas.

It just ... stops.

I look at Ricky and say, "Really, bro? Are you serious, man? You have a problem. Sometimes I don't know what's wrong with you, man."

He didn't have much to say to that, so we got out of the car and had to call his brother. Then, all we could do was wait because his brother, bless him, had to go out to a gas station, fill up a gas can, come out to where we were, and put the gas in Ricky's car. So while we're waiting, we're sitting on the curb of the emergency room parking lot. I'm sure we looked like quite the group: Ricky's out of gas, I'm out of patience, and Sam? Well, Sam is almost out of life.

As we're sitting out there, I guess the nurses and the doctors were paying attention and keeping an eye on us. After a while they came out to us and they said to Sam, "Hey, would you at least come inside and talk to us?" And surprisingly, Sam agreed.

He goes inside with the medics, and they start chatting with him. Meanwhile, Ricky and I are still sitting there on the curb waiting for his brother and the gas. And then we hear this sudden commotion inside. Ricky and I jump up and run back into the emergency room where we see people running around, moving carts, just doing all kinds of different things. And Sam isn't there. The nurse from before recognizes us and we go over to her asking after Sam and she tells us in a rush, "They're taking him into emergency. They've gotta pump his stomach."

I said, "What?"

And she simply replies, "Yeah. He told us what he actually took and it wasn't what you guys said. What he actually took is really dangerous and if we don't get it out of him, his liver will start to shut down and he could die. We've gotta pump his stomach."

Those medics got to work, and Ricky and I waited anxiously to see that Sam was okay. Thankfully, he was. They were able to save him, and he was fine in time. They got all that mess out and he recovered. But at the end of that day, Ricky and I stopped and just took some time to reflect on everything. We realized that if the Camaro hadn't run out of gas like it always did, we would've gone on back to that conference. And if we had, Sam probably would have died that day.

See, that day Sam gave up. He simply said, "I quit." He put a period at the end of his story. But lucky for him, and for us, he was interrupted by God's amazing grace. And that grace said, "No, a period doesn't go here. This is a space for a comma." And the Lord used a red Camaro running out of gas to be that comma—to save Sam's life.

If I were preaching right now, I'd say, "If you get it early, I won't have to preach as long." Well, if you get it early, maybe I won't have to write as long.

Jonah used a period. But God used a big ol' fish to be a comma, to rewrite the ending of that sentence and ultimately Jonah's story. God used a red 1995 Camaro to rewrite Sam's story.

You see, even when you quit on God, God says, "I haven't quit on you. You don't get to dictate the terms of how your story will end. You don't get to dictate what happens next. In this next season, I will use the most unlikely of things." For Sam, it was a red Camaro he did not want to be in. For Jonah, it was a big old fish he didn't want to be in. Maybe you are in something right now and you don't want to be there, but maybe it's a gift of God's grace. Maybe it's grace interrupting you, stopping your narrative, and helping you to see that God is up to something so much bigger than you could even imagine or understand.

God says that even in the fish, *I am here*. Even in a red Camaro, *I am here*. And His purposes will not be undercut by your unwillingness to trust in Him. God is saying to us, "When I go off-script, you may be done with Me, but I ain't done with you. I'll use the most unlikely of things, the most unlikely of places to bring about the power of My grace and bring it to bear in your life—in what you think is wasted time and seasons."

Now, speaking of time and seasons we view as wasted, I flunked out of high school. After that, the goal was for me to go to this junior college and work on getting my GED. I went and registered, and I signed up to major

in a trade while I was also fulfilling my GED requirements. It was a good plan, but it didn't really pan out.
The truth is, I never did fulfill those requirements in
that way. I just kept putting them off. I think I was
doing this out of a fear of failure. See, I didn't think I
was smart. I didn't think I could excel academically. I
knew I needed this GED to move forward in my life
and get a good job and become who I needed to be,
but I was struggling. In fact, every time I would muster
up the courage to actually go and take the GED test,
something would get in the way, and I just wouldn't
do it.

So many years passed.

All the while, I'm living for Jesus. I'm a Christian.
I'm working in youth ministry. I've preached my first
sermon. I'm speaking at youth days and youth confer-
ences, but I still haven't got this GED. So despite my
surrender and my declaration to follow Jesus, there's
this part of my life where I'm *still running from God*
and what He's called me to do. I'm just running from
this challenge because of fear and embarrassment, and
I'm not stopping. I'm just running.

But God met me. Long story short, an opportunity
came where I felt I could finally take that test and not
be hindered by shame or fear. A dear friend of mine,

Mrs. Connors, worked in the counseling department at the junior college, and she listened as I confessed one day about how I'd been running—from God *and* the GED. She listened and she provided me with a private space in her office where I could take the GED next time. I could be totally alone and in private and just do what I needed to. She offered this space to me, and I took her up on it.

Well, I'll never forget taking the GED that time and learning, weeks later, that I passed. I'll never forget celebrating with her and the immense relief I felt in that moment. But in the very next moment, I remember being hit with the burden of grief. All at once, a ton of regret fell on me. As I felt the joy of finally having that GED test behind me, I immediately thought about all the time I'd wasted.

All. That. Time.

Years. I had wasted years running from the GED and running from God. I had spent years running from this huge task in front of me. And now, with it done and accomplished, I just immediately thought about all the time I had lost—all the time that was now gone.

I'll never forget what happened next: Mrs. Connors cut me off in the middle of my tailspin. She looked at me and said, "No, don't you do that. God knew exactly where you were. He knows exactly where you are. And He knows exactly where you need to be. You haven't wasted any time. God's got a way of redeeming time, and you've been in His hands the whole time. This is the day that it needed to happen. This was the day when it was supposed to happen. Don't lament the loss of time because God has been faithful and He knows where you are, and He knows where you're going."

Immediately, I was so encouraged. I thought, "Yeah, I haven't wasted time. God's been keeping my time."

I'd imagine after spending three days in the fish, Jonah probably felt like he'd wasted a lot of time. But through his experience, he came to the end of himself and to repentance and was reminded of God's goodness, faithfulness, and sovereignty. And the fish, when God was ready to release Jonah, miraculously dropped him off right where he needed to be to board a ship to Nineveh. During those three days, God had instructed that fish to strategically place Jonah, when his "fish season" was over, right where he was supposed to be to fulfill the assignment God had given him.

The time spent in the fish was not wasted. That time was necessary for his surrender, but it was also strategic for his placement. Jonah hadn't lost time. He hadn't lost his place in line. He ended up where he needed to be, and he did so thanks only to God's strategic timing.

If you're feeling stuck, or like precious time has been wasted due to your running or resisting, I just want to encourage you. Your eyes have been opened. Grace has interrupted you. You've now seen that running is futile, but that doesn't mean the time spent running was pointless. Resist the temptation to lament and regret what feels like lost time. Know that God doesn't waste pain *or* time. You might feel like you did all the time-wasting yourself, but your God is sovereign and your time is in His hands—He redeems the time we call wasted. You just need to trust in Him. Don't spend good energy and focus on regret. Instead, use that energy to focus on the time gained and redeemed as you walk in the way of Christ and His Spirit. Your time in your Camaro, your time in your fish, my time not taking that test—it wasn't wasted. Our times were always in His hands.

So, yeah. God uses runners.

Now in chapter 3, Jonah, fresh from failure and on the way to recovery, is met by the Lord again. The first line of the chapter says, "Then the word of the LORD came to Jonah a *second* time." Now, this tells me something about God and how He doesn't give up on us. I just thank God for second chances. I thank God for chapter 3s in my life. When I get to start over, when I get a chapter 3, it really reads like how my chapter 1 should have. But it took Jonah two tries to get there. It takes us all multiple tries. I'm so thankful for the moments in my life when I got a second and a third and a fourth chance. God is in the business of offering us chances long after we deserve them. So, the Lord spoke to Jonah again in verse 2 and said, "Go to the great city of Nineveh and proclaim to it the message I give you." And this time, Jonah obeys the word of the Lord. He goes and picks up right where he should have in chapter 1. He goes and he preaches this word the Lord has given him and it's a powerful sermon. It's short. It's only a few words long, but the whole city experiences revival. The whole city repents. Even the king repents and the city renews its commitment to God.

Now, you've got to be a *bad* preacher to go in and the *whole city* repents. And I mean "bad" as in *really, really good*, in case you were confused. After Jonah's sermon, the whole city turns around. But don't get it twisted. This miracle probably had very little to do with Jonah himself. Jonah probably was an effective speaker, but the city's reaction is truly a testament of

God's love, truth, and faithfulness. It shows us that, more than anything, even when you run away from God, even when you don't follow Him, even when you try to control and manipulate Him so you can do your own thing, *God will still use you.* God will still use runners.

So, I hope this is encouraging. If you've been running and living outside of God's will and purpose for your life, if you found yourself out there going your own way, can I just tell you? God will still use you. Sometimes you may be thinking, "I've used up my chances. I've failed so miserably. I've gone off-track. I've gone so far out of God's way, will, and purpose. There's no way that God wants to use somebody like me..." But I'm telling you: If He'll use Jonah, He'll use you. And if He'll use Albert, He'll use you. He specializes in using people who have a tendency of running and doing their own thing. God used Jonah in a powerful, mighty way. God uses runners. I can't say it enough.

Now, remember Ricky? I know I told you all about his red Camaro and that we're best friends, but maybe I didn't say we're also cousins. Our great-grandparents are siblings and Ricky and his dad are in a long line of preachers. Ricky's dad, Richard Sr., is a third-generation preacher and Ricky is fourth-generation. Now, Ricky's grandfather was the pastor of my church growing up and Ricky's dad was just a great friend in addition to being my best friend's dad. So, we would often find ourselves over at their house hanging out and playing around. Well, over time I learned that Ricky's dad hadn't wanted to be a pastor or a preacher. He'd had no plans to do it. But he came from this long line of preachers and the calling on his life was undeniable. By his own admission, though, Ricky's dad ran for years. He was a musician in the church and would lead worship and often preached through music, but the whole idea of pastoring and preaching was not what he wanted to do for some reason. So, he ran. For years. Until one day, God got ahold of him.

It was January 23, 1994, when Ricky's father would eventually preach his first sermon, and everyone was excited because Richard had finally accepted his call. At 6:00 p.m. at Sweet Home Church of Christ Holiness USA in Pearl, Mississippi, Richard Jenkins Sr. would take to the pulpit and deliver his first sermon. I will never forget that day because that afternoon, another one of my best friends, James Sutton, along with Ricky, came to my house where we were having

Sunday dinner. Now, at our house, Sundays were always wide open, so it wasn't odd for someone to drop in, grab a plate, and join us. Ricky and Jamie came that day and they were just so excited as we all got up to greet them. Finally, Jamie, nearly bursting, says, "I've got a big announcement to make! Today I gave my life to Jesus."

Whoa.

We were all like seventeen years old at this point. Everybody in the house was just praising the Lord and it was an exciting time. Interestingly enough, the month before this, Ricky had given his life to Christ, too, through this powerful dream that he experienced the Rapture and was left behind. He got up out of his bed crying, went to his dad, and his dad led him in the prayer of salvation right there that night. So now Jamie, just that morning, gave his life to Christ. Ricky, a month ago, gave *his* life to Christ. Both of my friends looked at my mom and said, "Well, two down, one to go," and they were pointing at me.

At that moment I was thinking to myself, "Yeah, I'm good, y'know. I love Jesus. I'm good." But it was then that the Spirit of the living God arrested my soul. He started speaking to me and I knew that my time of running was almost up.

Run from Him

That night at six o'clock at Sweet Home Church, we all gathered there to hear Richard Sr. preach his first sermon. I was sitting in the back row with Ricky and some other friends of ours and throughout that whole service, I didn't hear one word. The entire time the Spirit of the Lord was just speaking to me and I remember, as Richard Sr. stood up to preach that first sermon, the Lord said, "Tonight is your night. When he ends this sermon and says, 'If you want to give your life to Jesus Christ...' I want you to get up, go down to that altar, and surrender your life."

To me, it was as clear as day. I knew that this was the moment for my full and complete surrender. So as Richard Sr. was preaching with passion, conviction, and tears, he came to the end of his message. He asked the question: *Who would like to give their life to Jesus Christ?*

In our faith tradition, the culture was that those who would come to accept Jesus didn't just raise a hand while they stayed where they were. No, you would literally get up, walk down the church aisle, and make your way to the altar. Like I said, I was sitting in the last row, and the church was packed. There was no way I could do this without being seen. So, I remember walking down the aisle and thinking to myself, "I'm going to go up there, get saved real quick, stop for a Blizzard from Dairy Queen, then go home."

So, I start walking and people start to notice me. They start to applaud and just raise up this celebratory noise. There was this moment—it was almost cinematic—where I'm just walking to the soundtrack of my church family's applause. The closer I get to the front, the louder the soundtrack is getting: people are clapping and shouting and whooping. The whole time I can feel this emotion rising in my chest and I say, "No, no. Uh-uh, we are not doing this today." And so I try to push it down. *Get saved, get a Blizzard, and go home.* That was my mantra. That's all I was doing—but the emotion kept coming up. And something happened when I passed that last row.

When I got to the altar, it felt like a four-hundred-pound weight was lifted off me. I fell into Richard Sr.'s arms and we both cried profusely as the salvation of the Lord overwhelmed me, overtook me, and completely transformed my life.

I'll never forget that day, January 23, 1994. And I'll never forget the preacher who, after years of running, said yes—because God used this runner to lead me to Christ. Thanks be to God for still using runners.

Angered by Your Grace

Now, like the first three chapters before it, the fourth chapter of the book of Jonah opens with a rather unexpected line. I have to say, I love the first lines of these chapters because they just give you a great insight into what's happening. For example, the first line of chapter 1 says, "The word of the LORD came to Jonah." The first line of chapter 2 says, "From inside the fish Jonah prayed." Immediately we know something went terribly wrong. But then comes chapter 3: "Then the word of the LORD came to Jonah a second time." And we understand that we get to start over. And now, chapter 4 begins with this unexpected line, "But to Jonah this seemed very wrong, and he became angry."

Huh?

What happens in the last chapter of Jonah for him to go from "I'm so glad to be alive and redeemed!" to "Now, this seems wrong and I'm angry." What is Jonah angry about?

Turns out he was angry at the grace of God.

See, the people of Nineveh were not nice people. Jonah didn't want to go there for an arguably good reason. They were known for being evil and oppressive.

They were known for developing innovative ways to torture humans. They had torture practices that were so heinous that nations feared and trembled at just the thought of this place and these people. They truly were evil. So, when Jonah is told to go and preach the grace of God to these people, he's afraid and he's skeptical. But as we know, Jonah makes it there. He preaches, and to his surprise, they all repent to the Lord, who was going to destroy them. In chapter 3 it says the Lord stayed His hand. He didn't bring His wrath upon them once they repented. He withheld the calamity that, honestly, they deserved. Instead, He gave them what they did not deserve: abundant grace. But Jonah sees God's hand of grace bringing about redemption and wholeness to these Ninevites and he becomes angry. He literally says, "This is why I didn't want to go there to begin with. I knew what You were going to do, God. I knew that You were going to give them grace. I knew that you were going to give these people an opportunity that, I feel, they just don't deserve. They don't deserve a second chance. They don't deserve access to grace as beautiful, holy, and righteous as Yours."

Jonah is clearly so angry at the grace of God and how lavishly He pours it out. Now, notice Jonah didn't have a problem with the grace of God when it was brought to bear on his life. He was fine with grace for *him*, but he was not okay with grace for *them*. We see that even now, after all Jonah has been through, he still wanted God on his terms. He wanted God to be better at following his, Jonah's, instructions. He still struggled with God's waywardness and disobedience, with God's refusal to be restricted by Jonah's expectations.

The fact that God would be so generous with His grace, not just for Jonah, but for those evil Ninevites as well, was out of the question. So, Jonah was frustrated. He was upset and unhappy and he felt like it was all unfair because what God was doing was not what Jonah would have done. Now, this shows us that one of the dangerous things about not trusting God when He goes off-script is that it reveals that we really want to be God ourselves. We really want control. We want to set the terms so badly that even when it comes to God's grace, we still want to be in charge.

Now, I've got one more story for you on runners, and this one is important because it talks about a runner's redemption: allowing yourself to eventually be caught.

In 1999, there was this screwball romantic comedy that hit the theaters called *Runaway Bride*, starring Julia Roberts and Richard Gere. It's a story about this beautiful woman who had gotten engaged. But on her wedding day, she just couldn't seem to go through with it so she took off running. The movie paints this story of her doing this time after time after time again. Now, Richard Gere's character is a newspaper journalist who hears about this woman and he's intrigued. He thinks her antics will make a great story, so he asks her for an interview and documents her life and her story. He follows her around and he's trying to understand why she keeps running away. And then he falls in love with her. She falls in love with him. They get engaged and there on their wedding day, you don't think it's gonna happen, but you begin to ask, *Will she run away again?* She's had a chapter 1, a chapter 2, and a chapter 3—and this is supposed to be the end of it. This is the big culminating chapter 4—the second chance. So, she's walking down the aisle. She gets close to Richard Gere's character. And then all of a sudden, the runaway bride strikes again. She runs.

But, unlike the other episodes, the other chapters, the other weddings, Richard Gere has a fierce resolve. He thinks she may run, but she will not get away. So he chases her and he chases her and he chases her and he refuses to let his bride go because he truly loves her and he knows she truly loves him. What I'm so thankful for is that we've got a God who refuses to let us run away without giving chase. He's pursuing us. He's running after us. He's coming for us. He is seeking us. He's a Richard Gere kind of God. So, even if you are a runner, even if you find yourself running away or just tempted to run, know that you've got a Father who will refuse to leave you. He's going to run after you because He refuses to leave you, and the people you will impact, graceless.

In the end, God writes Jonah's story, and while it doesn't end like I would want it to (with Jonah rejoicing at the faithfulness of God and doubling down on his obedience to God), it ends in what I think is a pretty realistic way. Jonah's story ends with him whining and angry at the grace of God, upset that others he deemed worse are just as worthy as he is of grace.

The book of Jonah doesn't end with a period, but with a question mark—because the end of Jonah's story is questionable. We just don't know how he ends up or what happens to him next. But we *do* know that God is right there with him. Even when Jonah tries to run again. Like the groom and the runaway bride, Jesus is right there. He is our Father in our runaway moments and He's right there refusing to leave us without a chase. And what's so beautiful about all this is that God keeps chasing—we just have to allow ourselves to be caught.

So if you're a runner, know that God is after you.

Know that no matter how far you go, He is right there, ready to follow, ready to receive you, ready to use you, and ready to redeem you.

As I continue in my conversations with my therapist, we keep coming right back to the same place. "Albert," he says, "where did you learn to respond like that? Why do you respond like that? And are there some new responses that you need to learn?" I guess as we wrap this chapter up, I just want to say to all the runners out there: When did you first start running? When did you learn to run when God shows up in your life to call you to places that, maybe, you wouldn't have signed up to go? When He allows a storm that wasn't on your schedule, what's your built-in response to Him? And if you're a runner and you tend to run away from Him, what would it mean for you to learn another response? What would it mean for you to retrain your intuitive reaction to God to be one of surrender and not of flight? Jonah would tell you that running from Him is a futile pursuit because there is no place where you can run where He's not already there. So take this as an invitation to go back to where it started and ask yourself, "Why do I run?" And then invite the Holy Spirit to show you a new response.

Chapter 3

Perform for Him

Everyone has a favorite talent competition show, like *America's Got Talent* or *American Idol*. One of my all-time favorites, though, is a show called *The Voice*.

The premise of the show is there are four chairs that the judges sit in, and the chairs rotate. That's a really important element because when a contestant steps out on the stage, they are looking at the back of the judges' chairs. Now, as the judges sit in the seats with their backs to the contestant, the contestant starts singing. If they sing really well and just do an amazing job, a judge will hit a button on their chair so that it will spin around so they can see who's singing because it means they're interested in them. If the contestant is so good that multiple judges turn their chairs around, then the judges have to fight over them, and ultimately, the contestant gets to pick which judge they want to work with as a coach to develop the contestant's singing career and, hopefully, launch them to stardom. It is the ultimate performance show because if you're performing blind, the judges don't see you or get to make any impressions that might sway how they feel about your singing. It's unbiased, and when you perform well, the judge(s) will turn their chair around and you will gain their favor.

Now, oftentimes when God is disobedient and goes off-script, there's a temptation to think something along the lines of "Well, maybe I can turn God around if I perform really well." In other words, if you perform in a very strong, meaningful way, then maybe you can get God to turn His chair around so you can gain His favor. I think we've all done this: we don't replace Him or run from Him, but in order to try to get a better response from God and for Him to align with us, we choose to perform for Him. We get on the stage, pick up the microphone, and we start performing in desperate hopes He'll turn around.

In Luke chapter 15, there's a story of Jesus sitting with sinners and tax collectors. The Pharisees, seeing Jesus keeping company with culturally irreligious people, begin to murmur under their breath and criticize Jesus for who He's chosen to spend time with. These people are, culturally, unbelievers. They're not on the "up and up." The undertone is that if Jesus, this would-be rabbi, is going to be spending time with anybody, it should be with Pharisees—the religious elite. You see, the Pharisees were great performers. They executed religion extremely well. They prided themselves on knowing the laws, keeping the laws, and writing new laws to keep. They were the premier religious community, and their posture would just reek of self-righteousness. They were the elite because, in their eyes, they were closest to God. So the idea of a rabbi or any remotely holy person spending time with anyone else, especially with people who lived so poorly and whose lives were marked by such low moral character and nobility—they detested the idea.

Jesus responds to their murmuring by telling three stories.

The first story is one of a shepherd who's lost one sheep out of one hundred and how he goes after the one that's lost. The shepherd eventually finds the sheep and brings it back to the ninety-nine. When the whole flock is together again, the shepherd tells his friends and they throw a party because the lost sheep has now been found and brought back to its community.

The second story is about a woman who has ten coins, but she loses one in her home. In order to find the missing one, she turns on all the lights and sweeps through the whole house to look for it. Once she finds the lost coin, she calls her friends over and throws a party to celebrate.

The third and final story is about one man who has two sons. In Luke 15:12, the younger of the two sons says to his father, "Give me my share of the estate," meaning what is owed to him through his inheritance. In other words, "Give me now what I would normally receive when you're dead." The translation there is that his son wants to live as though his father is already dead. Culturally, this would've been a huge insult because he was not just saying he wanted to live as though his father was dead, he was also living as if his father's way was dead to him: his father's values, instructions, influence, and way of life. Surprisingly, the father agrees to this, and once he divides up his estate and gives his younger son his inheritance, the boy loses no time moving out of his father's house so that he can live how he wants, outside of his father's way and will for him.

So as Jesus is telling this story, He describes how

the son goes out to a far country. Now personally, I like to call this place Vegas. I can see him pulling up to Vegas, pulling up on the strip, a pocket full of money and his mind ready for riotous and wretched living, if you will. He's got a lot of girls and friends around him. I see him rolling the dice at the craps table and everybody's just celebrating. He's got bottle service, he's got swag—he's got it all. It's this picture of him just being the life of the party and the center of all the action. And then Jesus tells us that when the son inevitably lost it all, all his friends were gone. When he lost, all the girls were gone. When he lost it all, he was left unto himself, fallen and a failure. And then? The younger son did what you should never do: he partnered with someone in this far country, in this Vegas, that he really shouldn't have—and it's a good life rule to never partner where you fall.

Well, he had indeed fallen. And he partnered with this citizen in the far country where he was and that person took advantage of him. The younger son soon found himself with no food, no resources, nothing at all. He was living in total squalor. The Bible says he was reduced to eating the food given to the *pigs*. Now, you have to understand: as a young Jewish boy, he would know that pigs should be just detestable and deplorable to him culturally. So for him to even be tempted to eat among the pigs—to eat what they eat—he had to be desperate. Because otherwise, such an act was unfathomable.

Now, after a while of living like this, the boy remembers his father. He came to himself and said, "I will arise. And I will go back to my father's house as a servant because the servants eat better than this." So he gets himself together. He goes, and while he's on his way to the father's house, Jesus says, the father sees him from a far way off. The father then runs to him. They meet in verse 22 and right when the son is about to grovel, give this apology speech, and negotiate the terms of his return, the father says, "Quick! Bring the best robe and put it on him. Put a ring on his finger and sandals on his feet." What the father does here is immediately tell his son, "No, you are not coming home as a servant. You're coming home as a son because servants don't have rings. Servants don't have shoes or wear robes. I want you to understand: you are coming home as my beloved son."

Meanwhile, the party preparations begin because once a son who was lost and now has been found returns, there has to be a party. Now culturally, there was a calf that had been intentionally saved and fatted for a moment like this. This calf was eating well and

84

waiting for a great celebration—it's literally called the fattened calf. So, when the father calls for this party, he says, "Kill the fattened calf! Call the community together! We are about to party and celebrate my son who was lost and has now been found!"

While this story sounds like it's all wrapped up in a happy bow, Jesus mentions the elder son and describes his reaction to his younger brother coming home to commotion and celebration: Hearing the party getting underway, the older son goes to one of the servants and asks what's going on, and the servant says to him, "Have you not heard your brother who was lost has now been found and your father is throwing a party?" And Scripture then says that the older son responded with great anger toward his father. He leaves, but his father follows him and asks, "Why are you angry?" And the older son says, "All my life I've stayed right here slaving for you and you haven't thrown me a party. Yet here your son, who has been living wildly in a faraway country, wasting money on women and goods, has come back home and you throw him a party with the fattened calf!"

The father gently tells his older son that he had to celebrate because the son who was lost had now been found. Because the older son was always with the father, he always had access to him, his love, and everything he owned. Yet, the story ends with the elder brother standing alone outside of the party.

Now, remember Jesus is telling three stories to Pharisees who have been critical about Jesus and the company He keeps. Keep that in mind because we're coming back to it quickly. Now, if you're anything like me, whenever you're watching a movie, you tend to identify with the character that's most like you. I do this all the time. Like, if I'm watching *Rocky*, I'm imagining that I'm Rocky. And after I've sat through a *Rocky* movie, I want to jump up and run up some steps. As a matter of fact, I remember when I was young, I did just that after I first saw *Rocky*. I started swinging, boxing the air, and then I started running up some steps. But then I realized, "Boy, you ain't Rocky. You're too fat to be Rocky," and I had to stop and go sit down and take a few pumps of my inhaler to get myself together. But the idea is that I identify with the character that most resembles me. And so Jesus, as He's telling these stories, tells them intentionally with His audience in mind. If He was talking to farmers, He would tell a story about agriculture so that they might see themselves in the narrative. While talking to the Pharisees, Jesus tells these three stories and I'd imagine that as they're listening to Jesus, the person they most identify with in the last story is the older son. Because, according to how the story is told, Jesus paints the older son as someone who does nothing wrong but still gets the short end of the stick—and that's extremely important.

Now, you have to keep the three stories in context: remember the first story was about a lost sheep that was then found, followed by a party. The second story was about a woman who had ten coins in her house but lost one. When it was found, she called her friends and threw a party. And the third story was about one father who had two sons. The younger son was lost and then found and the father called his friends over and threw a party. The older son was the only character in all three stories who didn't receive a party. So, as the Pharisees are listening, they're seeing themselves as the character who was left out and doesn't receive any celebration.

But—could it be that the first two stories are actually descriptions of the third story?

What if the first story is about the younger son? And the second story is about the older son? The woman had ten coins and she lost one. But where did she lose the coin? She lost it in the house. Where was the older son? He was in the house—and I would argue he was *lost* in the house. See, what Jesus was trying to get the Pharisees to understand and to see about themselves is that there are two kinds of "lostness." There's the younger brother's "lost" and there's the elder brother's "lost." The elder brother exposes his lostness with his anger at his father's grace and generosity toward his younger brother. Just listen to his opening argument: the elder brother tells his father in verse 29: "All these years I've been slaving for you." Oh, really? Slaving. Is that what it felt like? I thought you were here in the house serving your father because we were a family. You're lovingly coming alongside and investing in what we have as a family. But no, it didn't feel like that to the older son. It felt like slaving. It felt like labor. It turns out the younger brother and the older brother both wanted the same thing—they just went about it in two different ways. One left to get it and the other stayed home thinking he could work for it, perform for it, and earn it. And when he doesn't get it—when he sees the grace of his father given freely to his younger brother, who he thinks doesn't deserve it—his natural default is anger because he was entitled. Because all those years he was serving, he thought he was "slaving" so that he might get his father's blessing. They both wanted what the father had. Neither wanted who the father was.

So, what do you do with the disobedient God? With the God that you're trying to manipulate? With the

God who you're trying to get something from? Well, the older brother will tell you one strategy is to perform for Him. Do everything right. Do everything He asks you to do: church attendance, daily devotionals, giving away to the poor. Do whatever you have to do. Be a good person. Perform as much as possible so that you will be as good as possible because the better you perform and the more you slave away, then the better off you'll be. This way of thinking makes us believe that if we are always generous, on time, and disciplined in our Bible study, then maybe God will keep cancer from our home. Then maybe He'll keep tragedy from our lives. Then maybe He'll keep pain out of our children's hearts. In other words, "If I perform really, really well, then maybe, Dad, I could get Your chair to turn around and You'll give me what's owed me. Because the fact that the younger son got You to turn Your chair around, Dad, after all his destruction, and I've been here slaving for You all these years and You never turned Your chair around for me—it isn't fair."

An interesting part of this story is that the younger brother—everybody knew he was lost. There was no question that he was lost and that's why the whole community came out together to celebrate when he was found. Even the fattened calf was like, "Oh, he's back? Woo! All right, that's it. I'm dead. Take me out because this is the celebration we've been waiting on!" True story. Everyone knew where the younger brother was. But I think the most dangerous thing about those who respond with performance to God is that they're in the house and they're lost—and they have no idea. The most dangerous thing about a "fair say" approach is you can get it all right but still get it all wrong. You can follow all the laws, all the instructions, and still find yourself standing outside of the party, outside of the father's celebration for lost people, because you never saw yourself as lost. You never saw yourself as needing the grace of God to restore your life. You always saw yourself as entitled because whatever blessing you got, you earned it. You slaved for it. You labored for it.

Performers, be very careful. It's a very dangerous strategy because on paper you can be the epitome of religious success and still have the devastation of being a spiritual failure because you got it all right, but at the same time you got it all wrong.

While I was studying at Fuller Seminary in Pasadena, California, one of my favorite classes was an ethics class with Dr. Glen Stassen. Dr. S has gone on to be with the Lord now, but when he was here and I knew him, he was an excellent professor. He was a great, wise man and I really enjoyed his class. However, I have never been a good student in the traditional sense. I just have a different approach when it comes to academics. My strategy for success in class has always been unique and a little peculiar. See, you have those students who sign up for a class, go to class, buy the books they need, read the syllabus, and then follow the syllabus to keep up with the assignments. That's one type of student. I, on the other hand, like to walk in the Spirit and experience more of the Spirit's freedom. I like to study and just navigate academia, you know, with a more *Spirit-led* approach, if you will.

So, if there's an assignment and the Spirit shows it to me and reminds me, then praise God. But if not... well... See, when you choose to walk in this kind of freedom, you have to be prepared for some awkward, unexpected moments. There were times when I walked into class and saw people with papers on their desk and I realized, "Oh, we had a paper due today. Oh... I'll be back." And I'd have to leave and go do the paper. I'll never forget one evening when my syllabus just fell open and I noticed that I had a paper due soon in Dr. S's class. So, I knew about it early and I just praised God because the Spirit had moved.

So, I work on my paper and, y'all, I am so confident. I just know I've killed it. It was one of the best papers I've ever written. As a matter of fact, when I turned it in, I turned it in arrogantly—I threw it on the desk and I said, "Dr. S, you ain't even got to grade this one; it's an A waiting to happen." Well, I find myself in class a week later and they're passing back the papers and I get mine back and I'm looking around at my other classmates just shaking my head, thinking to myself, "If he grades this on a curve, you better believe I put the curve through the roof!" So, I'm just looking at them and everyone's reviewing their grades, and then I look at mine. Now, when Dr. S would grade papers, he would put comments on the front and your actual grade on the back. So, I'm already looking at the comments and I see on the front page of my paper in big red letters, "Great content!" And I'm thinking to myself, "I know! You ain't gotta tell me!" And then I go meandering through the pages just taking everything in and I get to the last page of my paper and there, in bright red, is an F. Scribbled under the F it says, "Wrong assignment, great content."

Wrong assignment.

You can live a flawless life—a life marked with spiritual sacrifice. You can seek to build spiritual fortitude, follow all the laws and the rules, and do everything that a "good person" or a "good Christian" is supposed to do. But one day, you're going to stand before God and He's going to review your life and He just may say, "Yeah, great content. You did it all right." And you'll be standing there proud, but then He'll say, "But it was the wrong assignment because I never knew you— and you never knew Me. You can know My rules and My instructions and still not know My heart." And, friends, that's what the father was inviting the older son to experience and celebrate. The Lord says, "This is my heart. My heart is of grace. My heart is of love. My heart is of forgiveness. It's not about the rules. It's not about performance. You've performed really well, but My heart was never about your performance. My heart was always, always about My love for you and My grace."

You can fulfill the wrong assignment. The assignment in life was for you to get to know God and to love Him and to live in the house with Him, not live in the house "slaving." You can miss a great opportunity to experience God when He goes off-script. He wants us to know His heart so that our reaction to Him isn't dictated by His behavior and how it measures up to our expectations—or our missed expectations. Your reaction to God should be built on His heart and the constancy of His love for you because He will lead you in His direction. When it comes to what we expect, or where we feel we should be or what we should be doing, we can miss God and His heart and His love completely. This is why one of the hardest things to really wrap our minds around is the grace of God. When you think about the grace of God, it just doesn't make sense and it just doesn't add up to how our lives are set up. Like, who does that? Who extends that kind of grace?

I'll never forget pastoring a small church in Mississippi and preaching and every week was just a grind. I mean, it was a hard task to study and to be ready to stand before people and articulate the truths of the gospel with compassion, clarity, understanding, and insight. Let me tell you, it was not an easy job. And it still isn't an easy job having to preach and prepare a sermon every single week. I remember this one particular week when I just hadn't prepared. Like, I just hadn't studied like I should; I hadn't prayed like I should. I was not prepared for the preaching moment. So, as I'm about to stand before the people, I'm praying before God, and I'll never forget this prayer that I was praying. The prayer was simply, "Lord, I'm so unworthy this week. I'm so unworthy. I didn't study like I should. I didn't pray like I should. God, I'm so unworthy..." And then I heard it. I can still hear it as if He said it today—I heard the Spirit of God speak to me and say, "Albert, when you studied all week, you still weren't worthy. When you prayed all night, you still weren't worthy. Your worthiness to stand and declare the truths of My gospel isn't based on your preparation. It's not based on your prayer life or the work that you've put in. Yes, it's important that you do that work, but don't you associate that work with your worth. Your worth was never your work. Your worth was always, always based on my work. All the work I've done in your life, it was always about *My* grace. It was about My grace on your worst day, and on your most prepared day. Either day, you're still unworthy. But what makes you worthy is My grace *alone*."

And it's so true.

Look at the younger brother: he is coming home, but he's not coming home with pure motives. The Bible says that the father saw him when he was still a long way off, and I would argue he was a long way off not just geographically, but theologically and spiritually as well. What was he doing? Why was he really coming home? Was he coming home to repent for what he'd done and be restored to his father's love? No, he was coming home the same way he'd left—trying to hustle a deal. He left with one hustle and that didn't work out. And now he's returning with another hustle. He's thinking, "I will go and be a servant for my dad because I've seen the servants eat and the servants eat better than I'm eating out here in these streets. So let me go home and negotiate a deal with Dad."

He's coming home to cut a deal. He still doesn't understand the grace of God. He still doesn't understand the love or grace of his father. He can't even wrap his mind around the depths of his father's love. He came home on a hustle, but he was met with grace— and that is so powerful. Some of us are coming to God with a hustle, but we are being met with His grace: "Quick, put a ring on his finger! Put a robe on his back! Put shoes on his feet." We see that the younger son may be coming home trying to hustle to be a servant, but his father is lavishing him with his grace so that he will be restored as a son.

So there we have it: the younger son was trying to hustle, but the elder brother was trying to perform. These are two responses we're all in danger of having. But the father said to the older son, "On your worst day and on your best day, all I have is yours. All you had to do was ask and I would've given you a party. You could have thrown a party. You could have had a party every day! Because the party isn't based on your performance—the party is based on *your father's* performance. *All I have is yours."*

The dangerous thing about those of us who seek to move the chair of God by our performance is you can get really good at performing. As a matter of fact, a mentor of mine once said to me, "Albert, be careful. There's a dangerous side to ministry." Immediately intrigued, I asked, "What's the dangerous side?" And he said, "The dangerous side of ministry is you can learn how to do it. You can get good at it. And before you know it, instead of pursuing the Father's heart through offering your gifts passionately, you can just become a performer offering up your performance, hoping that He'll turn around and be obedient to your instructions."

This is such a real danger and it can happen to any of us if we aren't careful. Jonah and the older son are similar. They actually have quite a few things in common: 1) They were both so angry at the grace of God that they found it really hard to celebrate. 2) They were both left standing outside of the party. The thing about performing for God is that, in a way, you're trying to manipulate Him, to get Him to align with your instruction and your will. And when you see Him move in other people's lives, when you see His grace freely disseminated and lavishly poured out on others, it makes you angry because you feel forgotten or left out. You're too busy thinking of all these years you've been slaving for Him. But He's saying, "I never asked you to slave. I just asked you to serve and to serve with your whole heart, mind, body, and soul. It was never your work that got you in the room. You've been waiting for Me to turn My chair around when what you've failed to realize is My chair was turned around *before you even got on the stage*. It was turned around before you even got in the parking lot to walk to the building with the stage! My chair was already turned around and My eyes and My heart were already set on you and I had already made a way. I was already standing up, giving you an ovation. It was never about your performance; it was always about *Mine*."

Chapter 4

A Tale of Two Fridays

One of my favorite holidays is Thanksgiving. It's when the family comes together and, I'm telling you, *we feast*. Now, being a Southern boy with a mom who had a special gift of hospitality, Thanksgiving was always a spread beyond spreads. Family members would come over and we would eat, laugh, play, pray, thank God, eat again, laugh, play, and pray some more. We'd gather around the piano and, since we're a family full of singers, we'd sing together and just have a grand time. We'd culminate the night with pound cake, homemade ice cream, and more singing of God's goodness, grace, and glory. By the early 2000s, though, the tradition was quickly changing. Instead of singing and feasting, we'd get to bed early so we could get up early and take advantage of the Black Friday sales.

Now, this isn't the case much anymore, but back in the early 2000s, it was becoming more and more common for stores to open at 6:00, 5:00, and even 4:00 a.m. with these excellent discounts. I remember flat-screen TVs were sold at great deals, digital cameras, iPods, and the latest iteration of the PlayStation—just all the electronics. So, if you got there early enough, you would just be able to get these popular items at a highly discounted rate for a certain number of hours—and this would create pandemonium. *Everyone* would be talking about these deals and they were all over the news, so there was no way to miss them. But, eventually, this became problematic. The pandemonium these sales caused got more and more out of hand each year and soon, tragedies were beginning to emerge. One of the worst tragedies happened in 2008 in Long Island, New York, at a Walmart. The store had advertised some really great discounted rates on a lot of great stuff and naturally, these discounts resulted in a huge crowd that was standing outside in the cold for hours waiting for the store to open. The workers would literally hold the doors and create a line for the shoppers to stay in until the opening hour struck. When the doors would finally open, the crowds would rush in and just begin grabbing everything and tossing it into their carts.

Well, on this particularly cold, crisp November morning on Long Island, when they opened the doors, it was chaos. Everybody came rushing in and in the midst of that mad dash to get through the doors, the worker who had opened the store stumbled, fell down, and no one noticed. He began to be trampled as all the customers were trying to force their way in before a coworker noticed, and though they tried to get the worker up, they just couldn't. The crowd had no control. After the horde of customers had spread through the aisles, the other workers were finally able to attend to their colleague unconscious on the ground. They had to act fast to get the man the medical attention he needed, but it wasn't easy: this Black Friday sale had created so much chaos at the store that they were literally trying to manage both the crowd and the crisis at the same time. As they were scrambling, they saw that this crisis had turned into a tragedy: the worker was dead. Realizing this, they tried to clear the store by going on the intercom, saying, "Please, please! We need space! We need you to leave the store! Something has happened!"

There was no response.

While they were still trying to gain control of the crowd, they said to one another, "Let's just be honest with them. Let's just tell them someone has died." And so they did. "Someone has died! Someone has died!" they declared over the intercom.

Later, in a news interview, one of the coworkers said the customers were like "savages." The interviewer asked, "What did they do after you told them to clear the store because someone had died?" The coworker looked directly into the camera and said, "They just kept shopping."

They just kept shopping.

Friends, this is the reality of Jesus. We have been consumed with shopping the aisles of the world. But there on Calvary's cross, there was a declaration and a decree that reigns all across the country and the world and throughout humanity that someone has died. *Someone has died*. Someone has paid a price so that we might live and yet we just keep shopping. We just keep shopping the aisles of the world.

See, the thing about Black Friday is that it is driven by scarcity. It's driven by this idea that there's not enough for all of us. Therefore, we're required to scratch, kick, fight, bite, push, and do whatever we have to do to get ours. There aren't enough DVDs for everyone. There aren't enough flat-screens. So, if you want to get the TVs, DVDs, iPods, or digital cameras, you've gotta do what you've gotta do. The value is for you and there's no value for one another. So, historically, fights would begin to break out at Walmarts and Targets that resulted in injuries and sometimes deaths, and these tragedies exposed our country.

When we experience scarcity, our values go out the window and we sin. Black Friday is fueled by scarcity, and scarcity can be used to corrupt us so easily. If you go back to the Garden, Satan gets Eve to doubt and eventually sin by asking her questions that give her the illusion of scarcity even in the Garden. What he begins to create in her mind is this idea of scarcity—this idea that God is hiding or withholding something from her. But the truth is that God has given more than enough. Still, Satan gets Eve to believe that the enough God invited them into was in fact not enough at all. In the midst of the greatest abundance. He said, "Did God truly say that you couldn't eat off that tree? The truth is, God knows that if you ate off that tree, you'd actually have more. You'd actually know all. You'd actually know of good and evil. You'd be like God." And although Eve was sitting in and enjoying ultimate abundance, the spirit of scarcity still got ahold of her and she started reaching outside of God's provision. She started long-ing for something outside of what God had provided. She was longing for God, but she started reaching out of the spirit of scarcity that Satan had created.

Now remember, it's okay to have questions. The issue isn't that she was questioning God or that she had ques-tions about His goodness. It's okay to have questions about God's goodness. It's okay to have questions when God goes off-script and when He's disobedient. It's okay to sit down and have such moments. So, no, the issue wasn't that she was questioning God. The issue was that she was questioning God while talking to a snake—and God was standing right there. God is always standing right there. When you have questions about God's good-ness, ask Him because He's standing right there. When you have questions about God's provision, ask Him. Because the reality is, God will always go off-script. He just will not be obedient to what you have laid out for Him. He will not exclusively give you what you want. That is not who He is. That is not how He rose. That is not what it means for Him to be God in your life. We have to recognize that even off-script, He's still God and He's still trustworthy. So when you have questions and concerns, it's best to process them with God.

No matter how it feels, the truth is that there's no

more scarcity because of the sacrifice Jesus made for us. We must open up our eyes to the abundance that is found in Jesus Christ alone. He's still sacred. He's still good. He's still faithful. He's still trustworthy. Even if He's delayed, even if *you're* delayed, you are not denied. He is a God who is faithful even if He doesn't fit in your timeline. When you open your eyes to His grace that is lavishly poured out—not just on you, but on all humanity—you have to celebrate. It's that moment when you realize there isn't scarcity—there is abundance. It's that moment when you realize someone has died, so why am I still shopping? What am I reaching for? It's that moment when our Black Friday meets His Good Friday. It's that moment when the scarcity of our world meets the abundance of Christ because He is more than enough.

I will not allow my missed expectations concerning His behavior to cause me to now miss the fullness of His glory in my life. He is more than enough. Regardless of His obedience to our instructions, we need to trust Him.

My grandfather was a pastor for forty years. He was a short man, but he loved to drive big cars. And not just any kind of car—he loved a big old Cadillac. You know, the Cadillacs that start at one end of the house and go all the way to the other end. Those Cadillacs where you didn't have seats in the back because you had a whole couch—and they didn't require seatbelts because they were made of such strong steel that you had to check whatever you hit, not the Cadillac itself. My grandfather had a long, wide, aqua-colored Cadillac that he just loved and he would pride himself on being able to drive it very long distances. Now, my family is from Mississippi, and all us Mississippi folks have cousins in Detroit. So, when we would go to see our cousins and our family in Detroit, Granddad always wanted to drive the whole way in his Cadillac. He prided himself on this feat because he ain't even have to stop for gas. The Holy Spirit would bring that Cadillac in on fumes.

Well, when I was seventeen years old, Granddad did something unexpected: he handed me the keys to his beloved Cadillac and he said, "June"—I'm Albert Jr.; now, Granddad didn't always have the energy to get the second syllable out, so he just called me "June"—and I said, "Yes, sir, Granddaddy," and he said, "I'm gonna give you the keys and let you drive, and I'm gonna shut my eyes." So, I climbed in the front seat and he got in the back. My grandmother was sitting in the passenger seat, my cousin Matthew was in the back with my granddad, and, y'all, I'm driving this big-steering-wheel Cadillac. So, we're going through the city streets heading to Detroit and I'm just driving, and it's been maybe thirty, forty-five seconds. Granddad suddenly said, "June." I said, "Yes, sir, Granddaddy." He said, "Now, son, speed this thing up. We want to get there before sunrise." And I said, "Yes, sir." So, I speed up. Then, in about another two minutes I hear, "June." I say, "Yes, sir." He says, "Boy, slow this thing down, son. We ain't running no race." I said, "Yes, sir, Granddaddy. Yes, sir." So, I slowed down. Then, after another few minutes I hear, "...June."

Now, by this time I could feel my grandmother getting irritated in her sanctified soul. She threw her arm back over the seat, turned around to look at him, and said, "Uh, I thought you said you was going to shut your eyes?"

See, my granddad had given me the keys. He'd even gotten in the back seat. But in his heart, he was still driving. Some of us, we've given God the keys and we've even changed seats and said, "God, you drive. You be in control." But in our heart, we're still driving. Sometimes I wonder if God peers over the balcony of heaven and looks at us and says, "Uh, I thought you said you was gonna shut your eyes?" And trust me, sometimes when God's driving, if I'm honest, He takes curves a little faster than I would take them. Sometimes He takes a turn that I would never take. Sometimes He'll drive down streets that I would never drive down. Sometimes He'll hit some terrain that's way too bumpy and rough that I would never opt into. And if I'm honest, there are many times when I am operating in what I like to call my own spiritual gift of back-seat driving and there's nothing more frustrating than for me to be trying to drive from the back. Still, He ignores my instructions and takes turns and goes at speeds I would never sign off on or sign up for. But maybe this is an invitation to acknowledge and recognize that He's God; He's not a seventeen-year-old kid trying to figure out how to drive. He's the Ancient of Days. He's the Alpha and the Omega. He's the beginning and the end. He's the creator of all things. So, maybe we should shut our eyes and trust Him, especially when He goes off-script, especially when He's not obedient to our instructions. Maybe it's an invitation. Maybe it's an opportunity to not allow the scarcity of our world to eclipse the abundance He's inviting us into. And oftentimes, we're inviting Him to be a consultant of our empire. See, He's a God of kingdom, but far too often, we're people of empire and we're trying to build an empire. And the thing is, we're not crazy. We're not irreligious. We have actually got some good theology because we don't want an empire without godly protection. So we're saying, "Lord, let me build the empire and you protect me because although someone has died, I'm still shopping these aisles."

But what we haven't even realized or fully internalized is that our Father is rich—He has a full kingdom for me and you and we don't have to hustle to get a discount from this world. We have abundance in His kingdom.

When Black Friday meets Good Friday, it redefines the whole relationship. This is the moment where you recognize that shopping the aisles of the world will never, ever satisfy your heart's deepest longings. And what Jesus Christ did on Good Friday is the only thing that could satisfy the deepest longings of my soul. So I recognize the shift between a world that calls me to scarcity and the kingdom that calls me to surrender so that I might experience the righteousness and the goodness of His glory. This redefining of perspective and our relationship with God is what this whole book is about. I call this chapter the "shift" chapter. This is the chapter where I pray the Holy Spirit would shift your perspective. If you've seen God as this disobedient

God, this God who goes off-script, this God who, inevitably, you can't trust, I hope that in this moment your Black Friday will meet His Good Friday. I hope that the scarcity of this world will meet the abundance of His love that He desires to transform your life with. I pray that there's a shift. And if you've been shifted, I pray that this serves as a reminder that *God is good.* God is in control. God is sovereign. So in whatever direction He decides to take and lead and drive my life, I will shut my eyes and trust Him because fighting the rat race of the scarcity of this world is not the purpose of my life. But to rest in the abundance of the goodness of God and all that He's done for me? Now, that's the purpose of my life.

Remember, this abundance does not mean there will be no storms. It does not mean there will be no hard times. It does not mean that there will be no crises, pain, trouble, disappointment, or even devastation. As a matter of fact, Jesus has never promised us a life without disappointment, pain, or devastation. But what He has promised is that when devastation, pain, and crisis come, you will never be alone. You have a God who holds all things and will make all things new and right.

Truthfully, there's a bigger plan that He's working

on and bringing to fruition in our lives, and it's bigger than this moment. It's bigger than this season. His plan is eternal. So although it might be hard right now, He's saying, "My son, my daughter—I know it's hard. Hold on to Me; trust Me. I am moving you toward the fullness of abundance and glory. We just gotta go through some dark valleys to get there. If you stick with me, I promise Good Friday and all its splendor will completely transform your life and bring you right to your purpose and your destiny." Truly, I believe this.

So this is the chapter that I pray the Holy Spirit shifts your perspective because, though He's wayward and disobedient, He is wholly trustworthy. Keep holding on, because your Black Friday, your scarcity, and your "not enough" are about to run smack-dab into God's Good Friday.

Chapter 5

Confess to Him

As we begin this chapter, let's start by asking a new question: What would it mean for us to trust God? And not just some vague idea of God, but the God of Israel— the God who has been faithful? What would it mean for us, instead of falling back to what's been familiar, to shift our eyes and trust our God who has been faithful? Specifically, trust Him when He goes off-script—what does it mean for us? What does it mean for our Black Fridays to surrender to His Good Friday? What does it mean for our feelings of scarcity to be overcome with His abundance, for us to walk in a grace that doesn't cause us to run or replace Him? That doesn't cause us to perform?

Well, there is an old practice that I think can help us in a new way: confession.

What if we just...confessed?

Confession

Confession began back in the book of Genesis, after Adam and Eve and the Fall. It began after they sinned by eating the fruit, but what they were really doing was reaching for something lesser when they were longing for God. They reached for the truth of the tree—for the fruit of the tree—instead of the truth and the fruit of God. And when Adam and Eve have sinned and fallen, there's this interesting dynamic that we see arise in the Garden.

Now, God is dominant and present and fully expressed. As we can see in Genesis, Adam and Eve could see and hear the Lord walking around in the cool of the day in the Garden. They had this intimate connection with one another—man and God, God and man. And then there's this moment where God asks Adam and Eve a question. He asks: "Where are you?"

Now at first, you gotta think, *where are they?* What kind of question is that? God, have you *lost* Adam and

Eve? The first children in the history of humanity and you've gone and lost the first set of kids?

But that's not what was happening.

See, it's not like God was saying, "Hey, have y'all seen them kids? Y'all—hey, Gabriel—where have the kids gone? Y'all seen them? Anybody know where they are?"

No. Funny and, let's be honest, *alarming* as that would be, God's not asking that question. He's not asking Adam and Eve where they are because He doesn't know where they are. He's asking them where they are to give them an opportunity to tell the truth. He knows exactly where they are.

You see, there's no place you can run where God doesn't exist. He knows exactly where you are all the time: He knows your brokenness. He knows your struggle. He knows your insecurities. He knows your desire to always compare yourself. He knows your temptation. He knows your lust. He knows your proclivities. He knows your sin. He knows your past. He knows your guilt. He knows your shame. He knows exactly *where you are* and *where you have been*. He knows it all, but there's power in that knowing. There's healing. There's something beautiful about you being honest with God about what He already knows. Because, even though He knows where you are, the question really is *Do you know where you are?* And are you ready to tell the truth about where you are? Because one of the greatest challenges of trusting and following God, especially when He goes off-script, is dealing with the disappointment, the missed expectation, and the devastation that we experience. In the nakedness of sin, failure, and disappointment, our first reaction is usually to hide—to try to cover how naked, exposed, and ashamed we feel. Because the enemy knows that if we can start hiding, if we can get shame to come over and cover us, the thought goes from "I can't face God or tell Him where I am because I feel bad about what I did" to something else entirely. Shame will say, "No, uh-uh, I feel bad about *who I am*." And then once you feel bad about who you are? Well, then the chances of you ever telling the truth about where you are become very, very slim.

So, confession begins with practicing telling the truth about where you are. This is what we do as disciples.

It reminds me of a story I love: the story of Thomas, the infamous disciple Thomas, the disciple often referred to as "doubting" Thomas. What's so fascinating about his story is that he gets labeled with that title and it is a point of failure for him. But I would argue that this "failure" is actually a point of empowerment and something beautiful that Thomas shows and models for us.

Now, some context in case you don't know or you need a refresher: The disciples have all gone through a lot. Jesus has just been crucified as an enemy of the state—as a criminal. Several of the disciples have literally rejected Jesus—some publicly. Some are just hiding and they're freaking out because they've just seen the fury of the Roman Empire and what that great, oppressive power will do to people who don't fall in line and worship Caesar. So, now they are the followers of the man who's just been killed. They are the disciples of Jesus Christ, who has been publicly crucified as a criminal. So, it's clear: They're all scared. They're all hiding in the upper room of the house they've gathered in—and it's like they're all locked away. None of them are trying to be known and seen by the Roman government. On top of that, most of them have doubts. Most of them are scared out of their mind. Many of them are fearing for their life. Thomas wasn't the only one who had doubts. Thomas was the only one, though, who was bold enough to say it out loud. He was the only one who would confess his doubt, but he wasn't the only one *with* doubt.

Oh, the beautiful gift of doubt.

We see doubt. We understand it. But the last thing we wanna do is talk about having doubts or confessing those doubts. But there's no way to avoid it. It's inevitable, especially when God goes off-script and we're left wondering what's happened and what's going on. When God is not clear? When you can't see clearly where He is or what He is doing? You definitely have doubts. It's a natural response. And sometimes there are seasons of following God when you've got more questions than you have answers.

You've got doubts, but don't allow the doubts to take over. Don't allow doubt to somehow discredit your faith, because the truth is that doubt is not a discrediting of your faith—*doubt is an acknowledgment of your faith.* To doubt at all is truly an affirmation that you actually have faith.

Now you may be asking me: "Well, Albert, what about atheists? Do you mean atheists don't have doubts? Atheists just don't believe to begin with, but if you're saying that the fact that you have doubts is proof that you actually have belief, then you're saying they, too, believe?" I may not be saying all of that. I don't know what atheists are or are not thinking. But what I do know, and what I am saying, is that doubt means you're struggling with your belief, and in order to struggle with belief, you first have to believe—right? So your doubt is, in fact, an affirmation of your belief and so, in a way, your doubt is actually a beautiful gift of belief.

That's right: doubt is a beautiful acknowledgment of a faith that you're wrestling with and you're fighting for.

And that's a beautiful gift.

It wasn't that Thomas didn't believe. It was that he had doubts and he was bold enough to confess them. God already knew he had doubts—Thomas just spoke them aloud. So, don't be ashamed. Don't be afraid. God can handle your questions. He's not intimidated or threatened by your inquiries, your curiosity, and even your accusations. He can handle your doubts.

Thomas, I would argue, doubted it in all the right ways. If you're gonna doubt, you should doubt like Thomas because, first of all, he said something about his doubt. You would be amazed at how many of us sit on doubts and we never say anything about 'em because we're too afraid to acknowledge and confess them. We never tell the truth about where we are. We always act like we've got to be more than we are, or we don't want to be the only ones where we are. So we just kind of . . . aren't honest about where we are. We just don't tell the truth.

But Thomas? He was honest about where he was. He said it. And what he inevitably learned was that he wasn't the only one in that place—he was not alone in his doubt. The others were feeling it, too.

One of the great strategies that Satan will use to get you to lock into your doubt and never confess is the embarrassment and the fear of you being the only one.

He tells you you're the only one who feels that way. You're the only one who had that kind of experience. Nobody else looks like they're struggling like you, so you must be the only one. And so, before you boldly stand and put yourself out there, just shrink and be quiet. Don't risk exposure. Don't reveal yourself to be the only one struggling because then that would indicate that there's just something wrong with you. The enemy tells you that this God thing works for everybody else, but there must just be something wrong with you. So before you are honest and tell the truth about where you are, you better stop it, hide, and then just fake it and act like you're there when you're really not. We've all heard the phrase *fake it till you make it*. Except you won't ever make it.

Thomas could have acted. To him it probably seemed like every other disciple had it figured out. They had unshakeable faith, total belief, and they looked like they ain't got no issues. He could've told himself, "Let me act like I got it figured out because clearly they all do." But no. Even when the disciples saw Jesus—even when Jesus Himself came back and showed them the reality of His resurrection—Thomas was like, "Yeah, I'm sorry. I...I don't believe it. You're gonna have to show me where the nails went in His hands. You're gonna have to show me." If you have the beautiful, beautiful gift of doubt, practice with it and the power of confession to say something. Tell the truth about where you are.

Now, the second thing we learn from Thomas is that he doubts in community.

One of the biggest things about life is that we struggle. We fail; we sin. And then, we run away from our Christian community. We run away from those who are designed to come alongside us and give us spiritual help and health. But can I be honest? I see why some of us run from these communities sometimes—'cause they ain't healthy. We've all been there. Some of these communities ain't marked by the Spirit of God and it's obvious. But when you find a godly community that's truly marked with the fruit of the Spirit, that's a place to lean in during your time of trouble. That's the place to lean in.

Sadly, when we have doubts and questions, I find so many people decide to just leave. They tell me, "I just left the church." But can I tell you that that's not the way to go? At least, not the way I see it or have experienced it. If you've got questions, that's the time you come to church. That's when you bring those questions and doubts to your godly Christian community so that you can wrestle with them, not alone—and not with those who won't help you.

You see, Thomas didn't go to the Romans or to the Gentiles. He didn't go to other folks or isolate himself. He doubted right there with his friends. He doubted right there in community. He doubted right there with the ones he had been walking alongside for three years.

Christian community is designed for doubts. It's designed for sinners. It's designed for people to wrestle. It's designed for people to fall and fail. It's designed for people to struggle and to still find grace, love, forgiveness, and restoration. Christian community should not be a place where we find self-righteousness, judgment, or condemnation. It should be a safe place for all.

So, what would it mean for us to become that kind of safe place marked by the fruit of the Spirit and the love and power of the gospel? What does it mean to become that kind of community for people like Thomas? For people like Peter? Even for people like Judas? What does it mean for us to become that kind of community? The kind that truly welcomes doubt, deconstruction, questions, accusations, and more?

Thomas found that kind of community.

It's important to note, too, that in his doubt and in his confession, Thomas wasn't looking for a way out of his faith. He wasn't looking for a reason to give up or walk away. He was literally looking for Jesus. And I find that so interesting because usually when we doubt, when we deconstruct, when we wrestle, so many times, we start looking for other things. We start looking for other solutions that aren't necessarily inappropriate but are out of priority. If I can offer some advice, I'd say, once again, to follow Thomas. If you're doubting Jesus, look for Jesus in your doubts. Don't just look for Him— look *to* Him. Search Him out and I promise you He'll be found.

So, I think it was appropriate for Thomas to say, "I don't believe Him. I need to see Him. I need to talk to

Him. I need to see where the nails went into His hands." And in Thomas's request, in his honest confession, Jesus was looking for him, too. Jesus met him there.

Now, I need you to use your spiritual imagination for a moment. I don't know if this is theologically correct, but in my mind's eye, I think about Jesus in His glorified body. And when I imagine that glorified body, He is healed. He's not bleeding. His skin isn't ripped open. Because the truth is, the crucifixion would have disfigured Him so significantly that He probably would've barely been recognizable when the disciples saw Him again. I imagine they clearly saw Him in this beautiful, glorified body and that caused a sense of awe and wonder for them, and not the fear and cringing a battered, crucified body would bring.

So, He has this glorified body where He's restored and healed. Which makes me imagine the angels and how they had likely tended to His body to bring that healing—and all of a sudden, they get to the nail marks in His hands and they're about to heal them and Jesus says, "Wait, wait, wait, wait. No—leave those holes."

And me? I'm thinking well, like, why does Jesus want to leave those holes? Why does He want to leave those marks in His new, glorified body? And then I think Jesus probably thought, "Well, you know Thomas is going to need to see something. When I see him, I want to be able to show him the marks in My hands."

In other words, Jesus made a way for Thomas's doubts. He already made provision for Thomas's questions. He knew Thomas. He knew what Thomas was thinking and He knew his reasoning. He knew that Thomas was gonna need to see Him, and let's be clear: it wasn't great that Thomas needed to see the proof. In fact, Jesus clearly said, "It would have been better if you believed without seeing, but today you need to see it."

That day, Thomas needed to see it.

And on the days when you need to see it and you don't believe it, God has grace for you. There's grace for you. There's a nail hole in His hand, because He knows that every day you won't believe it like you did, or every day you won't believe it like you should.

There's some days when you need that extra grace and provision and Jesus will not just bring it—He will offer it. You can doubt and He will bring grace, grace, and extra grace. So, if you're struggling in your beliefs, if you're struggling with your doubts, if you're frustrated with God, if He's gone off-script too many times in your life, if you're in a season where you've got more questions than you do answers, where you once believed but you believe less than you did before, can I encourage you? If you feel like the father in Mark 9:24 who wanted Jesus to heal his son only for Jesus to ask him, "Do you believe?" and the father said, "Lord, I do believe, help me overcome my unbelief!" can I say that I see you? If you're in a season where you said, "God, I've got some belief, but I've also got some unbelief tangled in there," would You help me and meet me halfway? Because I want you to know that you've got a God who has provided grace for your doubts, your disbelief, your struggle, your failure, and your shortcomings. He's provided grace because He knew that all your days won't be marked by great belief. Some days you've just got a little belief. Some of us, there are days when we don't have any belief *at all*. But, if He left the holes for Thomas, that means He also left the holes for me—and for you. Because He knew there would be hard days—days where we struggle to believe.

So, can we practice telling the truth about where you are? And not just where you are, but how you are and who you are? And can we take it a step further? The book of James tells us to confess our sins to one another. Confession is not a new practice but an ancient one, and one that has lost its significance in the church. Yes, we confess to Jesus, but James doesn't say confess to Jesus. He says there's also power in confessing to *one another.*

So what do you say? Can we do that? Can we put aside our fear and shame and our proclivity to hide and just be honest about where we are with one another?

Now, I want to back up a little bit. Remember how we talked about Christian community? And how, sometimes, that community can be a painful place? When James asks us to confess to one another, you may be feeling skeptical about how effective that really is. But the truth is that there's something powerful about confessing our sins to one another. But this ability requires us to feel safe with our Christian community. You want a community that is truly marked by the fruit of the Spirit—that is, the definition of love.

That definition is found in 1 Corinthians 13 and Galatians 5—you know the verses: "Love is patient, love is kind..." Well, this is true. Love is those things. And if you're in a Christian community that is not marked by the fruit of the Spirit described in Galatians 5, then it's also not marked by love. If you're not experiencing the description of love found in these passages, then I would argue that's not a healthy, safe Christian community and I would not bring my confessions to that place. You've gotta find a healthy Christian community because only in that place can you safely and genuinely confess your sins to one another.

Now, when I think of a safe Christian community, I think of my mentor, Pastor Bryan Loritts, who founded and started a multiethnic church in Memphis, Tennessee, along with several other pastors many years ago. I would always look to them for new innovative ideas and how they would approach the liturgy for Sunday. And over time, they began to do something called "Confession Sundays." Confession Sundays were a time when they would try to put into practice—in public gatherings—what James calls the church to.

They would literally just open up the mic, create an atmosphere of worship and adoration to God, and then invite brothers and sisters to come and publicly confess their sins to one another, just like James says. The church members would confess where they struggled, the places where the enemy had gained a foothold in their life, the spiritually depleted places in their lives where they so desperately wanted God to move because sin had taken up residence.

And you know what? It was beautiful. They would do these beautiful things—and it was *powerful*.

Confess to Him

So, I decided that I wanted to do this at my church. And I remember calling Bryan and asking him about it just to get the details, you know? Well, he says, "Yeah, we did it a few times, but my church is on punishment. We're not doing it right now." So, I said, "What do you mean your church is on punishment? You're not doing it right now?" And he says, "Well, last time we did it, there was a lady that stood up and she began to confess. And as she was telling her confession with tears in her eyes, she began to describe how, when she was a child, she was abducted by Michael Jackson on an alien ship. Michael Jackson held her hostage on a UFO and took her to outer space and wouldn't let her go. But thanks be to God, he finally let her out."

I'm going to give you a moment to pause here because I know I needed one when I first heard that myself.

Well, as the church listened to this confession of a Michael Jackson alien spaceship abduction, they all were in awe. Bryan and the church leaders were in awe, too, and they were wondering, "What in the world do we do now?" It may sound funny here, but it was a terrible, awkward moment. It totally derailed this time of confession. So, Bryan just closed in prayer in the midst of the awkwardness and *then*—if you can believe it—the band came up and played "Billie Jean," the iconic Michael Jackson hit, for the recessional. So, yeah. After that, Bryan decided the church was on punishment.

Fair enough.

Well, despite the awkward reality of what happened at their church, we gave it a try. I stood up and I talked about the power of confession and how James calls us to confess our sins to one another, and in order to create and set the atmosphere, I confessed first.

I confessed about my struggles with lust, with my own faith, and with trusting God to be all that I needed Him to be in my life. And then one of the most powerful things that I've ever seen began to happen. People began getting up, heading to the microphones, and just telling the truth about where they were.

I was astounded. I know you would think that this would be a common posture for a place of worship, for a church service—but it's actually not. Church services tend to be filled with people who look like they've got it together, who look like they've got it all figured out, like they have all the answers and no questions. But that day it was clear that that's not who the church really was. The church was filled with broken, shattered people on that day. They were honest about it. They were so open.

I'll never forget it.

One lady stood and she talked about her addiction to food and the shame she attached to her weight and her inability to do anything about it. She knew she was unhealthy, physically sick in her body, but her food addiction overwhelmed and overshadowed her whole existence. With tears, we applauded and celebrated her courageous confession. Up in the balcony in the top right was a man who publicly confessed that that morning he had considered suicide. This was going to be his last service before he took his own life. There wasn't a dry eye in the house. As the vulnerability of his confession broke us all and as he told the truth about where he was, we stopped everything, surrounded him, laid hands on him, and prayed that God would be enough for him—that he would experience the power of God's glory and healing in his heart and in his life.

Not too far from him, just a few moments later, a young woman stood, barely able to speak. We were able to make out enough to hear and understand that she was confessing having an abortion and the regret and the guilt that she felt. The room was overwhelmed—but not with condemnation or judgment. It was compassion. And that compassion poured out on her. Women circled around her unprompted and just began to lay hands on her and just love on her. Story after story, for almost an hour, people just stood and told the truth about where they were. And I thought to myself, this is church. This is God. This is community. This is what we're about. This is what it means to be a follower of Jesus Christ. This is what it means to trust God when He had clearly gone off-script in just about everybody's life in that room.

But this was our response to Him. This was our reaction to Him. We weren't running, we weren't performing. We weren't replacing Him that day. We were confessing and telling each other the truth about where we were in relation to our God.

The word "confess" actually literally translates to "the idea to say what he says." So, confession is the very idea to say of myself what God says of me. As I tell the truth about where I am, I begin to speak God's words about who I am.

So many times, we are so quick to wear the labels of this world. We readily wear the labels of sin, of not-good-enough. We say, "I'm not this" or "I'm not that." But a label isn't a label unless you put it on. Just think about it—if you don't put the label on, how can it define you? Imagine you walk into a place and they've got a bunch of name tags on a table. It only becomes your name tag if you take it and you wear it. So what would it mean for you to only say what He says as you practice confession? How would it be if you didn't put on anything that He hasn't spoken over you and about you? Don't wear anything that He hasn't written. If He didn't speak it over your life, let it go by practicing confession. Confess, and then say what He says.

Both sets of my grandparents have passed, so I no longer have living grandparents. A memory of my grandparents that stays with me, though, is, before they passed, finally getting to the place in our relationship and in my adulthood where I was able to go in every room of the house. The areas that were once forbidden to me were now open. I know it may be funny and strange, but as a grown man, I still took pride and honor in being able to walk into these formal spaces to just sit and be. I was humbled and overwhelmed with respect to finally be sitting in this space—to be welcome. As we close this chapter, I guess that's what I want to invite you to the next time God comes off as disobedient. When He shows up in a way that literally devastates you. He may not have caused this crisis or the pain that you're experiencing, but come on—we both know that in His sovereignty, He allowed it.

So what if the next time that happens, your first response is to boldly walk in the room of doubt, lament, and frustration, sit on the plush, beautiful righteousness of God, and confess to Him what you really feel. Confess to Him how you are experiencing what He has sovereignly allowed. And I'm telling you that that room is significant and substantial enough to hold your confession and take on your accusation. Because His righteousness, like my grandma's white couch, and His blood, like my grandma's red plush carpet, are still enough to cover, redeem, and receive your confession that at times may just sound like an accusation. The blood covers it all. So sit down, my brother, my sister, sit down in His righteousness; go into the room that may have seemed forbidden before. Now, though, with this disobedient God, come in this room of doubt and frustration and take rest—find rest because there's rest in your confession.

Chapter 6

Rest in Him

I'll never forget sitting in my Intro to Theology class and my professor introducing this concept about what belief is. He said, "Belief is made up of three things: the assent of the mind, the consent of the will, and, ultimately, the reclining of the heart."

So, let's bring that to John 3:16: "For God so loved the world, that he gave his only begotten Son, that whosoever believeth in him..." (KJV). Believe in Him. It's the idea that "whosoever" would have the assent of the mind (the understanding of who God is), the consent of the will (the willingness to surrender your will for His), and the reclining heart (a heart that would fully rest in who God is and what He's done through His Son).

Jesus Christ and the gospel aren't about what we do. The gospel is about what *He* has done. The gospel isn't an invitation for us to work harder; it is an invitation for us to rest harder in who God is and what He's already accomplished. It's this invitation to have your heart fully reclined in Him. So, this is the culmination of belief: to find that rest that brings us into eternity. In other words, in order for us to believe God, to trust God, and to follow God, we must inevitably rest in God by allowing our hearts to recline in Him.

So, what do you do with a disobedient God who goes off-script? My brother, my sister—you rest in Him. You accept the invitation for your heart to recline in Him. You don't just conclude an understanding concerning doctrinal truths and you don't just suddenly modify and change your behavior and say, "I'm gonna live differently." It's not that easy. It is a daily surrender. The beauty of belief and the power of the gospel is to find yourself fully reclined in Him. So our salvation is marked by belief, and if we understand belief as ultimately resting and allowing our hearts to recline in Him, then our salvation is simply to fully, truly rest in Him.

You remember the story I told you about my granddaddy? When he let me drive the car? Ultimately his decision to let me drive his car and his belief in me being able to drive that car were marked by those three things that make up belief:

Number one: The assent of the mind. He thought and concluded, "June can drive my car." He made a decision—the assent of his mind—to let me drive.

Number two: He gave me the keys—that's the consent of the will. He took what he thought in his head and he put physical action to it. He made a change in position and posture. He surrendered his keys to me. He changed his behavior. He's no longer in the front seat driving. He has moved to the back seat and he has said, "June, get in the front seat."

So, we've got two out of three so far: We've got the assent of the mind where he says, "I understand and I conclude June can drive." Then we've got the consent of the will where he handed over the keys and put me in the driver's seat.

But then we come to number three and therein lies the problem: the reclining of the heart.

Remember, when Granddaddy got in the back seat, he had done everything but recline his heart. I was driving, but he wasn't resting. And friends, that's the problem. When God goes off-script, we've got to not just remember but also *understand* who He is. We've got to recognize that there's a consent of our will, *and* we need our bodies and our actions to match our belief. We've got to trust Him. And if we trust Him, but we aren't resting, then we aren't actually trusting at all.

We see the blueprint for salvation and Sabbath with God and the children of Israel. He has delivered them out of the oppressive regime of Egypt and from under the hand of Pharaoh, where they were tortured and terrorized as slaves. God sent Moses to deliver the children of Israel after hearing their cries and their great moaning.

So, Moses spoke: "Let my people go!" Pharaoh refused. These plagues ensued.

They culminate in the Passover, and after this great triumph, the Israelites are faced with the Red Sea—but God parts it. So they walk across the sea on dry land and all of this is the faithfulness of God. He has done all of this. He delivered them from slavery. He brought them through the Red Sea and they're on their way to the Promised Land. But they stop in the wilderness and it is in the wilderness where God speaks to them and says, "Okay, I have loved you. I have delivered you. This is how you love Me back." And He does the "DTR." You know, He "defines the relationship." He lets them know how they are to live together as God and people in relationship. God says, "Let Me define love for you. I have loved you. I have brought you out of Egypt. Now let Me show you what it means to love a God like Me." Then He goes to the list, the commandments: "Thou shall have no other god before Me. Thou shall not make unto thee any graven image. Thou shall not create your own version of Me that should take the name of the Lord. Thou shall not use the name of God in vain— don't waste the power of My name." And then He tells them, "Remember the Sabbath day to keep it holy and set apart. Remember the seventh day and keep it different from the other days."

In other words, God makes it clear so there's no confusion. He says, "Here's how it works. Here's how to love Me. Here's how we work together. I want you to put into practice one day of the week that looks different from all the other days of the week." It's an invitation to rest. It's an invitation to live life differently.

So many times in our lives we work for rest. We work really, really hard so that one day we might rest, and God is saying, "No, there's a new rhythm. There's a better way for you to love Me and there's a better way for you to let Me love you. Instead of working for rest, I invite you to just rest."

Now, this was very hard for the children of Israel. They would really, really struggle with not working for a full seven days. This idea of having one day off, not doing anything that looked or felt like work, not doing things that would delight them and enrich their soul, was hard. But it was in this difficulty that he was rewiring them. Remember, the Israelites were under one of the most oppressive regimes in the history of humanity. They were slaves. They worked from sunup to sundown every single day. There were no breaks because this wasn't a job—it was enslavement. This lasted for generations, and they were so used to it. And now God is saying, "I need you to rest as I rested. I need you to take a day off so that you know you're no longer under the regime of Pharaoh. You are no longer oppressed. You are no longer slaves. I am not Pharaoh. I am the Lord, your God who loves you, who has made a way for you, who has brought you out."

The practice of the Sabbath is to remind you that you are not a slave to your schedule. You are not a slave to your to-do list. You are not a slave to work. You are not a slave to money. You are not a slave to your needs. You gotta stop. Because when you stop, you have no other choice but to recognize the world keeps turning because you are not God.

Rest in Him

If you were God, then when you stopped, everything would fall apart. It's amazing how often we work from that exact posture: if we don't make it happen, it won't happen. It makes us begin to take on this godlike view of ourselves that says, "I've gotta keep going, because if I don't keep going, the world will stop turning." But can I tell you, my brother, my sister, believe me—you are not God and nothing reminds you of that better than you resting, stopping, and refusing to keep going...and inevitably seeing that the world spins on. *God* is in control. And He is consistent. He is loving. He is merciful. He is faithful in all His ways. Shut your eyes, trust Him, and rest and remember you are no longer slaves. So let your heart recline.

You can't say, "I trust Him," and then walk in anxiety. That is not a reclining heart but a working worry. That's why when we accept Jesus Christ as our personal savior, He invites us into this eternal rest that we get to practice right now. Yes, we will have eternal life, but that eternal life starts today. It's not something that just happens when we die and go to heaven. Know that eternity starts right now in the reclining of the heart. It's in that belief that rest truly starts and God is so gracious that we get to begin practicing now with the Sabbath.

Now, this all sounds great, but unfortunately, the children of Israel missed it. While they were still in the wilderness, they complained and worried so much that they ended up missing the rest God called them to. This is why in Hebrews 4, the Bible says there remains a rest because there was a previous generation that didn't experience it. They missed it. And I guess therein lies a warning: Although God has rest for us, we can miss it. We can find ourselves roaming in the wilderness instead of resting in His provision and His promise. We can miss the rest. God wants us to rest as He rested. He created the world in six days and on the seventh day, God then rested. The seventh day was marked for rest.

Now, you've got to ask the question "Why did *God* rest?" Did He rest because He was tired? Did He rest because He needed a nap or a break? No, God is not like us in that He gets tired. He doesn't need a nap. The Bible says He rested because His work was completed. He rested because He was finished.

The invitation for you and me is to rest from our work so that we might rest in what He has finished. When we come to the end of our work—when we recognize that it is not about our work, but about *His* rest—when we come to the end of our ways, our will, and our works, that's where Sabbath begins. God wants us to practice it every seventh day.

As God invites us to Sabbath, He talks about the power of His word. He describes it in Hebrews 4:12 this way: "Sharper than any double-edged sword, it penetrates even to dividing soul and spirit, joints and marrow; it judges the thoughts and attitudes of the heart." It's this imagery of the word of God exposing every part of us and here we come back to confession—acknowledging the good, the bad, the ugly. The word of God judges righteously. It looks and it evaluates and it declares righteous or unrighteous, good or not good. It brings opportunities to grow and be stretched. The word of God gives you a metric by which to measure your life and—if you allow it—it speaks to your attitude, your decisions, your choices, your habits, and your practices. If you allow it, the word of God gets to the innermost parts of your being and tells you the whole truth about who you are and where you are.

I don't know about you, but if the word of God has done all of that on me, then I'm not feeling secure. Honestly, I'm feeling embarrassed and ashamed because I'm not proud of some of the stuff that's gotten exposed. It's some stuff that I'm not cool with and that I don't want nobody to see—especially not the high priest of God.

But He says, "I'm not a high priest that you can't have access to. I'm a high priest that knows what it's like to be you, because I put on flesh and I lived among you." So He knows what it is to be tempted and to struggle. He knows what it is to have our experiences, but He went through them without sin. So in His judgment of us, He's not judging and condemning as the world does; He judges as a high priest who knows, loves, and understands us and invites us to be better in His presence.

When you are seen and—in some ways—exposed, it's hard. You probably feel embarrassed. You probably feel ashamed. You probably feel insecure or like you need to perform to be better. You may even feel proud or arrogant. But He doesn't want us to feel pride over what's been exposed. The truth is that He wants us to come to His throne of grace with boldness and confidence, not shame, fear, or guilt. Resting in Him means trusting Him, and trusting Him means lifting up your head and coming into His presence with boldness.

One of my favorite pastors, Dr. Tony Evans, tells the story of how he and his wife were on a cruise ship when it hit turbulent waters. The ship is rocking and the captain tells everyone to go back to their cabins and stay there for the remainder of the evening. Well,

Dr. Evans talks about how his wife's frustration was at an all-time high because they had paid for this expensive cruise and weren't planning to spend any part of it locked away in the cabin. So out of her frustration, she calls the captain to have a word. Except she doesn't get the captain—she gets an assistant, who takes a message. She says, "Listen, I have a couple of things I want to express to the captain. Number one, we paid a lot of money to be on the ship and we don't wanna be locked in our room. How long are we gonna be locked in this room? And number two, are you even able to navigate these waters safely in this storm?" See, she questions his credentials and his ability to navigate this storm. She goes on to say, "I'm gonna be up tonight unable to rest because I need to know how long these turbulent waters are going to last and whether or not we're going to be okay."

The assistant says she'll take these issues to the captain. In time, the captain sends a message back to the assistant to give to Dr. Evans's wife. It says, "Number one, go to sleep because I'm going to be up all night navigating this ship and if I'm gonna be up all night navigating, there's no need for you to be up worrying. Number two, I don't want you to just go to sleep, I want you to rest easy and be assured that when naval engineers designed this ship, they did it with storms in mind. It's equipped to handle it."

I guess the invitation to you, my brother and my sister, is to know that your life was designed with these kinds of storms in mind. God created you fully knowing these moments that would cause you to question His faithfulness, His moves and decisions, and His sovereignty. He knows you were going to question His goodness because He's allowed things in your life that have now created storms, disruptions, and even devastation. I want you to know you should go to sleep and you should rest in Him and you should rest easy because your life was engineered, orchestrated, designed with these kinds of storms in mind.

So, friends, get some rest.

So many times during this pandemic, I heard people say and wonder aloud, "Wow, what if this is a big test that God has given us?" People looked at 2020 as the year of being tested. God slowed the whole world down: Freeways were clear. There was no traffic in Los Angeles. Venetian water canals were sparkling clear. In many ways, I thought that while lockdown was one of the most difficult times, it was also a time when

God was answering some of my most challenging, difficult prayers. I wanted to spend more time with my family. Check. I wanted to spend less money. Check. God answered these prayers I had about wanting a lifestyle that felt slower and a rhythm that felt healthier. Check.

Now, the challenge came when the world started to open back up. Traveling became normal again. Going in stores and shopping was something you didn't have to rush through or totally avoid anymore. Even removing the mask was an option. Well, one day I was talking to a good friend of mine, Aaron Lindsey, who's a pastor of Believe Church LA, and he said, "Albert, I don't know about you, but I feel like God gave me a real gift during the pandemic. He gave me rest and a healthy rhythm in a time where, you know, let's be honest, He allowed something that no one agreed with. No one thought this pandemic was a good idea, but in God's sovereignty, He allowed it." So we are wrestling with a disobedient God who's gone way, way off-script. But in the midst of this we're both talking and we're just expressing how God answered so many of our prayers. And could it be that not only did we want the answers to our prayers, but we also wanted to define the geographical locations in which our prayers would be answered? Not only did we want the prayers answered, but we wanted God to show up in a certain kind of way in a certain kind of place. And God in His sovereignty allowed this pandemic to slow us all down—and He still answered our prayers in a world crisis.

Aaron Lindsey then said something to me that I'll never forget. I've been saying it to myself and to whoever would listen ever since I heard it: "What if the pandemic wasn't the test, but it was the lesson? And what if now is the test to see if we can stay on rhythm in a place of rest with God?" On this side of the test, many of us have found that what we valued so much before the pandemic has now changed. During lockdown we valued family, community, gathering, conversations, and quality time. Can we still value those things? Now when the world is back wide open, I guess God is saying, "Okay, here's the test. Even when I'm disobedient, can you still rest in Me? Even when I've got you in a place you never would have signed up for, can you still take time and trust Me enough to rest in Me? Can your response to My disobedience, to My sovereignty, to Me being a God who refuses to compromise My will because of your passionate desire be one of rest, and not running? You don't replace Me. You don't perform for Me. But, come here, you rest in Me and allow Me to be the sovereign God I am. I'm faithful and I can get you through a hard time."

Now, will you pass the test? Will you be consistent in finding God as your place of rest?

Chapter 7

Reach for Him

Leading an organization has its rewards and challenges. I've been leading our church for over ten years and my leadership skills have been stretched considerably in that time. We began as a small startup and now we're so much larger than I or anyone else imagined. Through it all, I find myself learning more and more about myself and paying more attention to my own leadership and how I understand what that is and what it needs to be. The biggest lesson I'm learning in this latest season is to pay attention to my response *to* leadership. The first time I noticed this was a couple of years ago, and it was actually because it was pointed out to me after we'd hired a business consultant. See, you can pastor and preach, but that doesn't mean you know how to lead an organization, with all the financial and interpersonal elements that come with it. So, I was trying to grow in organizational and administrative leadership and learn how to build a healthy culture between myself and my staff.

Well, at one point, someone who worked in the church just did something really frustrating. I mean, it really ticked me off. I was disappointed and angry and I honestly didn't want to have to work with that person anymore because of it. I decided I needed to reposition them in the church so that we wouldn't have to cross paths. So, as I'm working on restructuring the staff to get this person away from me, I'm also processing all of this with the business consultant we'd hired, who happened to be a Black man from London and also a great friend of mine. I'll never forget his accent and how it just made everything he said sound so smart and reflective. Well, as I was processing with him, I asked him what he thought about my plan to reposition this staff member. He simply said, "Well, what do you think?" So I said, "What do you mean 'What do I think?'" And he said, "Well, what do you think about that decision?" Now, I'm just not understanding, so I looked at him and he looked at me, and then he said in his proper English accent, "I think what you're doing will be reactive and punitive." Now, if I can be real, I thought to myself, "Dang right it will be! That's exactly what I want it to be!" But then I realized what he was saying—and what he was doing. He was pushing me to pay attention to my response to this situation. He wanted me to see my own reaction. He gently called attention to the reality of my response in a way I could see and understand: I *was* being reactive and punitive. He was right. What I was trying to do was actually wrong—but the crazy thing is that it felt so right. It was my most natural response and it made the most sense to me to retaliate in this way. But it was still wrong.

He pushed me to see that just because something might be natural, it doesn't make it noble or necessary. So, just because that's my natural response, it doesn't make it right. My response shouldn't feel reactive. It shouldn't have been punitive. He taught me to think about my built-in response and what actually needs to be expressed to show respect and dignity to those around me.

I had another opportunity to learn this thanks to an encounter with one of my peers on staff—a young lady who was expressing a concern that I had a completely different perspective on. Our differing opinions created this tension that led to a rather confrontational conversation. First, she said something hard to me. Without thinking, I reacted to what she said, because at the time it felt like she was just asking for a reaction rather than a well-thought-out response. Like I said, things were tense. And see, I knew she wasn't going to like my response, but she was asking for it. So, I gave it to her—and the conversation just didn't go well. It went poorly and ended even worse, to no one's surprise. After this happened, I was trying to learn to be a better leader. I didn't like how things went and I wanted to know how to not just fix that one bad conversation, but to make sure it didn't happen like that again. So, I processed with one of my coworkers, Michael Field, who is also a dear friend and a dynamic pastor at our church. Now, Michael is a nine on the Enneagram—you know, the peacemaker. He's a reconciler, and honestly, everyone loves him. Now, I'm an eight on the Enneagram, which means I can be angry and disruptive. Everybody loves me, too, but they've got to love me at a distance. But I want to be loved like Michael. I start thinking, "How do I get people to love me closer like Michael?" So, I called him up and gave him the situation. I gave him a play-by-play of what happened between me and the staff member. When I was done, I said, "Now, tell me, Michael. What? What just happened?" I let him know that what I was looking for was some perspective on how I could have handled that conversation better because while I wanted to push back against this staff member, I wanted to do it in a way that was just... better. Kinder. More conducive to a favorable outcome. Well, I'll never forget what he said because it stopped me in my tracks.

He said, "Well, when she said that, you could have just responded by saying, 'Thank you for expressing that. Give me some time to think about it and I'll get back to you.'"

I remember thinking that never in my life has it *ever* crossed my mind to say something like that. The thought of *not* expressing what I think and feel in real time has just never occurred to me. I've never considered delaying a response because the question is almost always "What do you think?" And I always know what I think at that moment. I don't need to stop and figure it out—I've never had to. But just because I know what I think "right now" doesn't mean that I know how to properly express that thought or feeling right now.

Michael helped me to see the necessity of not just having a reaction, but taking time to create a well-processed, thoughtful, and healthy response. We as people need to experience a healthy response, not an immediate action. We need to slow down—stop, wait, and think. But what did it mean for me to slow down? I began to learn not just how to do it, but how to pay attention to my reactions and then invite the Holy Spirit into the process of cultivating a healthy response. Your reaction doesn't have to be the raw, emotional response you have and process through therapy. There's nothing wrong with that first, natural reaction, but it shouldn't be unleashed on someone just because you feel it right then and there. Through a great community, I'm learning to ask my soul an important question: "What are you?"

Now, let me set that up a little bit before I get there.

See, these experiences have helped me to understand certain things about myself. If I have these emotional reactions within myself, then I'm probably doing them to more than just my coworkers. I'm doing it with my friends, my wife, and maybe I'm even doing it with God. Could I really be doing it with God, too? Short answer: Yeah, I *am*.

It's amazing how many preset responses and reactions I have. In short, I've been programmed.

Let me say that again.

I'm amazed at how many preset responses and even

reactions have been programmed in me. With God? It's amazing how when He frustrates me, I quickly reach to replace Him with other comforts: food, sleep, television. It's amazing how when He calls me to do hard things, I immediately reach for my track shoes so I can run from Him. And sometimes, when I'm really guilt-stricken and I'm really trying to get Him to move on my behalf, I'll get on that stage and I'll just start performing for Him in hopes that He'll turn His chair around and see me.

Far too often, I reach to replace Him. But I'm learning to not allow my reactions to difficult things to become my response to Him. I'm learning to ask my soul, "What are you reaching for? What are you longing for? Can you tell the difference?" When we're experiencing isolation and loneliness and we're longing for God but we're tempted to reach for pornography, we have to stop and ask what's happening with and in our souls. "You're feeling anxious and worried because you're longing for security that can only be found in God but reaching for it in the world. Soul, what are you reaching for? What are you longing for?" And when I ask my soul these questions, I'm having to pay attention to what it says back to me and what those responses actually mean.

So, I'm daily inviting the Holy Spirit to reprogram me—to reprogram what I reach for when God goes off-script. When I don't feel His nearness, sometimes I start to grab things that bring numbness rather than satisfaction. I mean, I'll look up and before I know it, I'm responding to my God with this reaction that may be all natural, but still all wrong. Because no matter what we're feeling or going through or longing for, the answer to what we're *actually* looking for is always God. It's always God. Our souls are always wanting God.

In Scripture, King David had access to everything: money, wealth, women, fame, anointing, power, authority, and personal talent. He had it all and he failed a lot. He wasn't perfect by any means. But he's given this compliment by God in 1 Samuel 13:14: "The Lord has sought out a man after his own heart." That's right. Scripture refers to David, this man who has failed and sinned and racked up quite a record, as *a man after God's own heart*. What a compliment. What a showing of great love and respect. For me, though, anybody who gets that level of compliment from God Himself causes me to pause because I want to know, *What did he do?* "What did he do when God was disobedient? How did he respond to God? What was his worship like? What was his life like? What was the posture of his soul? How did he process his reaching and his longing?"

Psalm 27:4 gives us a glimpse under the hood of David's heart that helps answer some of these questions. In it, David simply says the following: "One thing I ask from the LORD, this only do I seek: that I may dwell in the house of the LORD all the days of my life, to gaze on the beauty of the LORD and to seek him in his temple."

The first two words of this psalm always stop me in my tracks. He says, "*One thing* I ask..." One thing. When I read that, my first question for David is, how in the world, with all that you have around you and all you have access to, did you get your desire down to *one* thing? How did you get yourself to the place where you wanted one thing only? Because, speaking as a man who doesn't have nearly as much as David, part of my problem is that I don't want just one thing. I want *all* the things. I want everything I'm supposed to have. I want everything I'm *not* supposed to have. I want the things other people have, and I'm frustrated by the things they have that I don't. I want *all the things*. But, somehow, David narrows it down to just one. He says the key to worshipping, trusting, and following God when He goes off-script is that you have to get your heart down to one thing.

In other words, we've got too many desires. We've got too many priorities. We've got too many things that are shaping and driving our passions and pursuits. David says, "I only wanted one thing. I only desired one thing. I got my heart down to one thing." To get a glimpse of that one thing, I suggest we look to Psalm 23. Here David is writing as a shepherd boy and he starts the psalm with these three words: "The Lord is." Now, we can stop right there.

"The Lord is," David says. "The Lord is...all that I could ever need. All that I could ever want. Out of all the things in the world, it is God who sustains me. God who is my portion. The Alpha, the Omega, the beginning and the end. He is the first and the last. He is whatever I need whenever and however I need it. The Lord is all that I could ever desire. And all that He is, He is all that *in me*. Because I've invited His business to be my exclusive business, I shall not want. Because if He is all, that means I am not. I am not at the center—the Lord is. And because of all that He is, I shall not want anything outside of what the Lord has provided. So, the Lord is my shepherd because He is the Lord." And that was the key to David's heart. He only wanted what God wanted. His heart only desired what God desired. And he says, "If the Lord does not provide it—if the Lord does not want me to have it—then I have trained my heart not to want it, either."

David conditioned his heart daily to only desire what God desired for him and to only long for what God longed for him. And then he says the one thing he has desired of the Lord is the one thing he will seek: he will exclusively reach for the Lord.

What an example that is for us. A man who had everything sought just one thing with his whole heart: the Lord. So, how do we apply that to our own lives?

My daily seek is my daily reach. What I desire, I will reach for. I train my heart to reach for what it reaches for. And if I want that to be God, I must daily surrender, train, and condition my heart to reach only for God.

One thing have I desired of the Lord and that will I reach after: to be in His presence so that I may dwell in the house of the Lord.

You see, if I'm sitting in His presence, then I'm sitting in His provision. If I'm sitting in His provision, then I'm resting in His promise. If I'm resting in His promise, that means I'm following His plan.

Lord, I want to be where You are. I want be in Your presence. I want to dwell in Your house. I want to sit under Your influence. I don't ever want to leave. I don't ever want to live like You don't exist. I want my life to reflect Your life. I want all that You are to be all in me. And I want to do this for how long, Lord? All the days of my life. I don't just want to visit You. I want to reside with You. I don't want to just come see You on big holidays or in moments of crisis. I want Your presence to be my dwelling place. I want Your house to be my resting place. I want to be where You are, and while I'm there, I want to behold Your beauty. I want my eyes to be so fixated on Your beauty and my heart so enamored with Your glory that all of my inquiries will be right there in Your presence—in Your temple. I don't want to go outside of Your beautiful presence. I don't want to reach for anything outside of Your temple. You're the only place where I shop because You died and made a way for me to gain access in this beautiful place called Your presence. I'll only shop in the places You've provided. I'll only inquire in Your temple. The Lord is my shepherd. Therefore, I shall not want anything that the shepherd is not providing.

So, I'm daily practicing what it means to get my heart to one thing. And it isn't easy. I'm daily inviting the Holy

Spirit to reset my programming. I'm daily inviting the Holy Spirit to reprogram my responses and reactions. I've been in this sinful flesh for a long time, but the Holy Spirit can change even my most basic proclivities and responses to match God's heart—especially when I don't understand God's heart because it's gone way, way off-script. In my life, three specific things have come up recently that I don't understand and are off-script: autism, diabetes, and uncertainty.

A little bit over a year ago, our youngest son, Micah, got diagnosed with autism. This is child number four and my wife, LaRosa, and I have always had a clear script for what our kids' lives would be. We had detailed hopes and dreams for their abilities. We had a narrative. We never wrote it down, of course, and I'm not even sure if we ever even talked about it out loud, but I know we had one. Because, when autism showed up in the script for our youngest boy, we had no room for it.

We didn't expect it. We would never have intentionally written it into the narrative that we're writing for our family. God just went off-script. He went off the plan. I mean, from the very time Micah was born it was clear that complications from his birth had delayed his development. Those delays were inevitably identified as autism. We both were just blindsided. We cried out to God, "What in the world are You doing? This is not what we planned!" But through it, I'm learning. We're learning. When God was disobedient concerning the narrative that I wanted to write for my family, it pushed me to learn how to really shut my eyes and trust Him. I'm finding that God's ability far exceeds my restrictions or the assumptions that I have about certain things. God can use something like autism in my son to bring glory to His name. Just because I can't currently see it doesn't mean it's impossible. So, I'm learning to trust Him. In this instance of our lives, we're way off-script—but, God, You're faithful. You're faithful. So, instead of reaching for anxiety and worry, I'm reaching for You. One thing will I desire and that's to be where You are, and if this diagnosis is where You are, may I, too, be found there.

In the beginning of 2022, I went to the emergency room because of a kidney stone. While there, I discovered that during my bout with COVID over the holidays, I had become a full-blown diabetic. Something about COVID pushed me over the edge, and I knew I immediately had to make a life change. So, I got to work. I transformed my eating and my lifestyle, but boy, I did not write any of this in my script. Because though I'm stable and have got this under control thanks to the lifestyle changes I've made, even now as I write this, it is still so scary and hard dealing with some of the complications and discomfort that come with high blood sugar and high blood pressure. There are things I can and cannot eat. It's difficult finding the right energy and managing the pain and discomfort in my legs and my feet. This is just not something that I wrote in my script. I had a full plan for this year—for the next five years. It did not include anything like this that would slow me down, that would change the direction of how I even practice life and my rhythms. I didn't schedule any of this. Out of all the prayer requests that I've offered and provided for You, God, this was not in one of them.

But here it is.

You've allowed something in the story of my life that I did not make room for. So, I'm daily learning to trust You and to accept the areas of this life that are marked by Your sovereignty and Your love, but also with my disappointment. I know You don't cause bad things to happen, but in Your sovereignty You allow them and I'm learning to trust You in what You allow in my life. I'm also learning to thank You for coming to me a second time. Like Jonah, we sometimes (or oftentimes) bring stuff on ourselves, and when we do, it's just so much easier to blame You because You're responsible for it all. But if I'm honest, there are a lot of poor choices that led me to this place of discomfort and disruption. So, I thank You for the grace to even have doubts and struggle with Your sovereignty. You still give me a second chance. Even in the midst of a hard diagnosis, You offer second chances. So, I'm going to keep reaching for You. I'm going to keep longing for You because if there's one thing that I desire greater than perfect health for me and my family, it is Your presence. Because when I don't have perfect health but I've got Your presence? Then I've got all I really, truly need. One thing have I desired, Lord. May I seek it daily.

Now, uncertainty? I feel like with the pandemic, the economy, racial upheaval, and the overtaking and overcrowding of elephants and donkeys in our society, it seems as if we're becoming more political by the day and less kingdom minded. Like, way less. And all of this has caused me a lot of anxiety and uncertainty. By the minute, being someone who's called to pastor a church and lead Christians in this day and age seems less than ideal. It seems marked with a high level of uncertainty. It seems like it's getting harder to navigate mental illness as it reaches an all-time high. Marriages just don't seem to last like they used to. Relationships seem to be strained more easily. People come to me seeking answers and guidance to these problems, and often I'm just uncertain of what to do or say.

On top of all that, the internet and social media seem to be marked by more evil than good these days. We know that Jesus' greatest prayer was for our unity, but it seems as if Satan's greatest ploy for our disunity is making a lot of headway. He's unleashed a strategy that seems to be working all too well. So, God, most of the things that are happening in culture and in society, I would not write. I would not put these things in my story. I would add a few bad things because that's life, right? But the things that are showing up now? I would never write these things. I would not approve of them if You asked me. I wouldn't cosign them. It just seems so hard and so challenging on so many levels for so many people—but here You are. You've allowed these things to be added to the story. You've allowed dynamics in the script that, let's face it, no one wants.

But even in that I'm learning to practice patience in

the midst of evil, disruption, and devastation. I'm practicing patience and confession, and I'm telling the truth
about where I am. It's so tempting to hide. It's so tempting to not be honest about how I really feel and how I
really struggle with the direction that You're allowing.
I am like Thomas—struggling and doubting and having a hard time with these hard realities. But, also like
Thomas, I am seeking You.

You see, what I want more than a world without
struggle, more than a healthy economy without reces-
sion or inflation, more than everyone avoiding conflict
and not having disputes, more than a world without
illness, more than all those things, is to simply *be with
You where You are*. And if where You are is in the midst
of challenging, confrontational, difficult times, then
that's okay. So long as I'm where You are and I can
still see Your beauty, I'll keep pursuing and inquiring in
Your temple. I'll find You even in a strange land. Even
in a hard, difficult place, I'll keep pursuing You.

I guess what I'm trying to say about this great question
of what you do with a disobedient God who goes off-
script is that there are many answers, but also one: You
reach for Him. You confess to Him, you rest in Him,
you trust in Him. Daily, I'm learning and relearning

these rhythms because when all is said and done, they are what you do with the disobedient God.

May we confess to Him.

May we rest in Him.

May we trust in Him.

May we reach for Him.

Postlude

What About Your Friends?

Have you ever heard the iconic song "What About Your Friends" from the nineties? The young hip-hop group TLC came out with this song that would become a summer classic in 1992, and honestly, it's a word.

The lyrics say something to the effect of "Will your friends be around when you need them?" In other words, do your friends have your back? Are they down to help you no matter what? Today I often think about how to live this out, but with God. I consider how to live in a way where I trust God despite the turns He makes and the decisions, calls, and devastations He allows in His sovereignty. How do we stay faithful when we're hurt and disappointed? How do we keep our heart set on Him? How do we keep our heart dialed in to the one thing? How do we daily reach for the one who we're longing for? We do it with friends.

Author William T. Ham says it this way: "There are many things you can do alone, but Christianity? Christianity is not one of them." So, one of the things you need to consider in order to walk faithfully in your longing for God is simply your friendships. It's something that we don't realize a lot, but your friends will play a huge role in your spiritual fortitude in life. Your consistency, your faithfulness, who's speaking into you, who's pushing you, and who's encouraging you all depend on who you surround yourself with. The book of Hebrews refers to it as this idea of having community and family and a church that can spur you along for good works. The idea there is to literally push you along toward good works and good decisions. So, you've gotta ask yourself, who's in your life who can literally push you around to purpose, destiny, and hope? If you've got a great heart and a great desire but got bad friends, then you've got a setup. That's just a dynamic waiting for disaster. So, how you choose and who you choose to be your sounding board and your community are so incredibly important. So, who's in your ear? Who are your friends?

Postlude

Job is a good example from Scripture. Job's community was important to him. However, while we give them credit for being there in a very difficult time in his life, how Job's friends showed up for him proved not to be very spiritually helpful. See, Job lost all that he had. God allowed him to lose it all. Satan desired him to lose it all in order to test his faithfulness and his loyalty toward God. So God yielded His hand and allowed calamity to hit Job's life. And when Job was at the bottom of the pit, his friends came over and the bottom of the pit got lower. His friends brought accusations toward him. His friends said, "Job, did you do something wrong?" His friends didn't know how to show up well, and Job felt the absence of the power of having great friends in that moment. What does it mean to have friends who push you to the God of hope in your moments of despair? And I don't mean hundreds of friends or even tens, but a few friends that in your most intimate, challenging, burdensome moments, you know you can call on them and they'll be present to listen, to sit, and to understand. And then, when you're ready, these friends will push you, challenge you, question you, and inspire you. Everyone needs this kind of circle. Even Jesus needed this kind of circle. He had the twelve disciples, but when things got tight, he had a tendency to pull away with just Peter, James, and John, and say, "Guys, I need moments in my inner circle with my close friends."

Who are your close friends? Who are the people in your life who can help you live out what it is to be a faithful follower of Jesus Christ, especially on the days when it's hard to follow Him, because He's not going in a direction that you would've ever predicted? Who's there to encourage you and to help you stay on task in your commitment to following Jesus Christ?

Personally, I pride myself on having really good friends, but it was really hard and challenging to fellowship with one another during a pandemic. As we were suffering grief and loss and experiencing all kinds of dynamics—family, job, community, even some health issues with bouts of COVID, and death—it was just hard. Now, friendship is based on being there and being present. Sometimes being present calls for great celebration and bottle popping. Other times it calls for grief and tears and silence. So, I found it very difficult to cultivate my friendships during this time, mainly because it was just hard to be physically present with one another. I had one friend who was going through a devastating time with his family—his daughter had made a suicide attempt, but, praise God, it didn't come to fruition. Still, I can only imagine discovering that your daughter has that level of struggle and crisis in her life to that degree and not knowing what to do—and not having your friends around you in that particular trench. We talked on the phone. And I could tell just from talking to him that he was having a very hard time and he needed his friends. But with so many different things going on and the risk of COVID, it just didn't seem like we would be able to get in a room together. It just didn't seem like we'd be able to find the time on the calendar to be together. But on the inside, I knew what he needed was not a Zoom call, or an encouraging text. This was one of those moments when he needed presence. And we just couldn't do it. So before we got off the phone, and conceding to the fact that we would not be able to get in person with one another, I remember saying, "Well, when the dust settles, man, we really gotta get together. When the dust settles, we really gotta hang."

I got off the phone and I just began to think about all the things that he was going through, all the burdens that he must have been carrying, the probable insecurity of his own fatherhood and what it must have been like to sit in that kind of pain and loss with his daughter. And I just remember thinking, instead of waiting for the dust to settle, let's just hang in the dust. So, I got in my car, canceled everything I had, and we spent the whole day together. We just hung in the dust amid the complexity, the challenge, the disruption, the crazy schedule, and the discomfort of disappointing people we were supposed to be with that day. We just hung in the dust.

If you gotta walk with Jesus, it's going to get dusty. The winds are gonna blow. It's going to be cloudy. You can't create a rhythm where you wait till the dust settles to be present for one another. You need friendships where you can hang in the dust. It's one of the ways we survive. It's one of the ways we thrive in following a disobedient God. Friends who walk with us, push us, challenge us, and yes, hang with us even in the dust of God's sovereignty help us through. God's sovereignty can be a challenge and a formidable force to wrestle with. It's this idea that God's in control of everything. So even if He didn't do it in His sovereignty, He allowed it. And how do I find rest in that? How do I find peace in that? How do I resolve that? You've got to develop a trust for God, but as you do so, remember that He's not intimidated by your questions or your anger.

Job will tell us he went and he saw God's sovereignty in what He allowed in his life. And Job took God to task. He asked Him, "Why did You allow this? Why did You do this? Why did You allow that?" He brought question after question and accusation after accusation. And I love it—in the book of Job, God finally speaks, and He says in chapters 38–41, "Job, are you done now? You've asked Me questions. Now let Me ask you, 'Where were you when I established the heavens and the earth? Where were you when I carved out the mountains? Where were you when the ocean was set in place? Where were you?'" God calls on His sovereignty and says to us, "In the midst of your crisis, trust My sovereignty. Know that even though you don't understand My ways or My will, I am good. You weren't there when I created the world. So there may be something about Me that you don't understand. There may be parts of My will that you won't grasp. Even if I showed you My plan, you still wouldn't understand. So there has to be a trust in My sovereignty. There has to be a rest in My sovereignty because inevitably I am in control and I am a good father. I will never leave you nor forsake you. No weapon formed against you shall prosper. Greater is He that is within you than he that is in the world. I am good and My will is good and My ways are good. So trust My sovereignty. Trust the fact that even though you feel out of control, I am still in control. I am sovereign. Trust Me. Trust Me."

Now, this may feel like a left turn, but I've got to take a moment to talk about something: the Peloton. I know what you're thinking: I'm about to go on a rant about the power of the cultlike members of the Peloton community with these bikes and these subscriptions and all of that. Nah, that's not where I'm going with this. No—we recently got a Peloton and my wife seems to love it. I haven't tried it yet, but the Peloton for me means something a bit different and quite a bit deeper. See, a few years ago I invited some friends to come hang out in my backyard around the fire pit. These friends were all pastors married with families—just in the same season of life. And we were sitting in the backyard talking—but honestly we were talking about the struggles and the burdens of life. You know, the ones that take out marriages and even careers for pastors. We talked about moral failure. We talked about the temptation of success and the struggle with identity and finding places for authenticity and honesty where you can just tell the truth to one another about what's been a burden in your own life in ministry.

As we were sitting around, we all acknowledged and expressed a need for that kind of honest space, that kind of community of truth-telling and safety to protect one another. And a friend of mine who was there referenced the word "peloton." Apparently, this is a French word and it describes a pack of riders during a bicycle race who group together because the more cyclists you have riding around you, the better energy you have during the race. There's also something about the split-streaming of the ride—it helps everyone go faster. So in many bike races and contests, cyclists would create a peloton—a group of riders to ride around one of the main competitors to help that main competitor go faster.

So, that night around the fire, we committed to riding alongside one another in a "peloton" so that together through accountability, confession of sin, encouragement, and support, we might all move faster. We might all get to the finish intact with no moral failure and no burnout.

We asked each other, "How can we help each other finish the race?" But the real question was, how could we help one another stay on task? And since we've made that pact, all of us have had our disobedient God moments: moments where something happened in our life that we didn't see coming, that we didn't expect, where God went off-script. And those were the moments where we rallied the pack and got the peloton. Together we move through challenges in our marriages, with our kids, with our jobs, with our churches.

We ring the bell when the crisis hits and the pack circles up, and we ride together. It's one of the ways to survive—one of the ways to thrive. Even in our pursuit and our journey with following God, with all the curves and turns and slopes that come along, this ride is a ride we take together.

I encourage you, my friend, to find your peloton and commit to it. You'll ride faster. You'll arrive better and you'll follow God more closely because that's what we do for one another. We push one another to God, even when He's disobedient.

We've Got a Good, Good Father

I can still remember the first time I heard the Christian hit song phenomenon "Good, Good Father." I'd never heard the song before and oddly enough, my introduction to it would be in Angola Prison, the Louisiana state penitentiary. That facility shaped a big portion of my life. I talked about it in my previous book, but hang with me for a moment. I remember the first time I got there. It's a huge plantation—just acres and acres and acres of land—and on this land are these buildings, these prisons. They have barbed wire, electrified fences, and these guards, and as you look at the land, you see prisoners working in the field. Angola is known for being one of the bloodiest prisons in the country, but on this visit, revival broke out there.

The warden allowed New Orleans Seminary to come on the campus. They started training pastors and then these pastors started planting churches right there in the cell blocks, right there on the grounds. And once these pastors started preaching and reaching, the bloodiest prison in America became the most blood-washed prison in America. The testimonies of what God has done in this place are absolutely remarkable, but I cannot even begin to express the trepidation that I felt walking on these grounds for the first time. You see, per capita, most of the men in Angola are doing life sentences, and they're doing them for either violent or sexual crimes. So as you do the math, you understand that most of these men have either murdered or attempted to murder or raped or attempted to sexually abuse someone. And this was my audience. So, as I come in with guards with guns, walking through multiple doors where buttons have to be hit before you're released to go into the next room, I was a little fearful. A little insecure is an understatement. But I'll never forget that something happened as we were walking down those halls and through those great metal doors:

we started singing Zion songs. We started singing about the faithfulness, the kindness, and the love of God—and the atmosphere just started to change.

And then I started to preach. And let me tell you, as I began to preach the word of God, these men were hungrier than any audience I'd ever experienced before. They were so hungry. They were receiving the word and shouting it back to me. They were so engaged and I thought I was in revival. Then, it happened: I did an altar call and many of the men came forward, either to rededicate their life or to give their lives to Jesus. It was this amazing move—this outpouring of God's Spirit. And then Matt Long, who was the worship leader at Willow Creek at the time, came to the platform and he started playing this chord progression that I'd never heard before. He then began to sing these lyrics:

Oh, I've heard a thousand stories of what they
*   think You're like*
But I've heard the tender whisper of love in the
*   dead of night*

And the men came in, joining along with the chorus. They sang it out: "You're a good, good Father." Just all these men, hundreds of men, declaring the goodness of

Postlude

God right there in Angola Prison in the chapel room. It was so surreal. I was surrounded by hundreds of incarcerated men who were all guarded by correctional officers holding guns. But even then I looked around and I was at home. I looked around and the goodness of God's sovereignty was so evident. Many of these men would never see the light of day again. So many would never get out of prison again—yet there we were with the spirit of joy and exuberance and excitement about just the thought of God's goodness. And you just have to ask the question: How in the world can God be so good in a prison? How in the world could God be so good while you're serving a life sentence? How in the world could God be so good in a place of confinement, restriction, and violence? How is the abundance of God's goodness so evident in a place like this? And, honestly, I would argue that these men had learned to rest in His sovereignty and not their condition. They were not resting in their circumstances or situations, because they understood that fundamentally God is good.

We cannot allow our circumstances and our situations to dictate our gratitude and our confidence and rest. And as we close this book, I hope you noticed an invitation to be reminded to rest in the sovereignty of God by not allowing your circumstance or your situation to define your posture of praise and gratitude toward God for the life and the situations that He's allowed you to experience.

I can't think of a room more prone to be depressed, discouraged, and devastated in, but there I was in the middle of life. People who have been marked by life crisis, people who are in the one place no mother ever wants her child to be, were there declaring the truth and the power of God's goodness. You're a good Father, even in hard circumstances and situations, You are a good, good Father.

Dreams, Rest, and Peace

So, we know that as we follow Jesus, the winds and storms will come. The challenges will come, but you can still rest and trust in Him. Jesus is qualified, and in His sovereignty, He is God and He is good. He is faithful. He is well able to navigate any storm that arises, and even if He was driving the ship that brought you into the storm, He's qualified to navigate through it. Not only should you trust God's qualifications and His sovereignty, but you should rest easy knowing that when He designed you, He did so in His image—in the Imago Dei. He made you with this kind of storm in mind—so you were built with this kind of storm in mind and can weather it with Him. He's not surprised, panicked, or in a crisis over the storms that have shown up in your life. He built you for them because He built you to be with Him. And we've gotta rest in that knowledge and truth.

But sometimes, people can't rest on their own. They take sleeping pills to help them. But Jesus is saying in order to sleep well, you need the peace pill. Now, I'm not pushing drugs in this book; I just want to make that clear. But you need a peace—and He has a peace. The letter to the Philippians talks about a peace that actually passes all understanding, and that peace will then guard your heart and mind through Christ Jesus. When the storms are hard, when the challenges are great, He'll give you a peace that doesn't make sense. He'll give you a peace that doesn't match the storm that you're in. He'll give you a peace that passes all common sense in all understanding. In other words, by any other translation or interpretation of your season, you should not have joy. You should not have peace. You should be consumed with anxiety. But God has given you something that doesn't make sense. He's given you a peace that doesn't match your storm. He's given you a peace that doesn't match your situation, but there you are. You've got a peace in the midst of a crazy storm. You got a peace that doesn't make sense. And that peace, as you navigate and go through this rough season, will stand as a guard. It will stand right in front of your heart and guard it so you don't lose heart. It'll stand right there and guard your mind so you won't lose your mind. So, I pray that the peace that surpasses all understanding in seasons of difficulty would guard your heart and your mind.

Now that we've got that out of the way, I remember sitting with God in a recent prayer time and just having to acknowledge an overwhelming sense of wonder because God had answered so many of my prayers. I remember pastoring seven people for five or six years, and God grew my little church there in Pelahatchie, Mississippi, to fourteen people. I remember going out and having to preach to such a small crowd and saying, "Lord, oh one day, if I had two hundred people." And then when I started my church in California, several years later, our first Sunday we had over six hundred people in attendance. God blew my dreams out of the water.

I love telling the greatest story that's ever been told. I love preaching. And I love the impact that happens when you tell someone the gospel story and their eyes are opened. I remember getting on a plane for the first time thinking, "Oh, I am doing what I was born to do. This has been my greatest dream. I would do this for free for the rest of my life!" And now I'm being invited to go to other parts of the country to tell this story. So I'm getting on a plane to go to another place and to tell people this story and I just remember thinking, "I can't believe I get to do this. This is a dream come true." And over the years I've been able to preach to hundreds of thousands of people and I just think, "Wow, I'm a long way from Pelahatchie. I'm a long way from those fourteen people." Now, to be clear, I learned to be faithful whether that was seven, seven hundred, or seven thousand. God was faithful, but I just remember when I was young, my dreams were to tell the gospel story to people all across the country and even all across the world and to build a great church to disciple brothers and sisters in the Lord and see people come to faith. And I just remember realizing one day before the Lord in prayer, "Oh my goodness. All of my dreams have come true." And I'll never forget it: I heard the voice of the Lord say, "Well, now that we got that out of the way, maybe now we can start focusing on some of *My* dreams for you."

Wow.

God says, "I'm glad you got your dreams done. Now let's take the rest of your life and let's focus on My dreams." It's a flip in perspective. It's a change of posture with ambition. It's this idea that my life isn't about God blessing me to fulfill my dreams. My life is about God blessing me to fulfill His so my pursuit isn't for my own vision, my own plan—it's for God's visions and plans.

Jesus would be proud of all these things. I think He would think that they're all great ideas, but the ambition, the core, the driver, isn't *Lord help me fulfill my dreams*. The ambition and the driver is *Lord make my life fulfill Your dreams for Your glory*. And may that be the driving force in our lives in order to trust and follow Him regardless of where He leads. You've gotta start praying a new kind of prayer so that your heart will match His heart.

Psalm 37:4 says, "Delight yourself in the LORD, and he will give you the desires of your heart" (ESV). So many times I've thought that prayer was about me getting what I wanted. I would think, "Lord, if I delight myself in You, and if I enjoy You, and if I live in You and my purpose, then whatever I desire, You'll just give to me." But now I don't think that's what that passage is saying at all. It's saying, when you learn to live in the Lord, delight in the Lord, then your heart will become like His heart and so what God desires, you will desire. Going back to Psalm 27:4, David says, "One thing I have desired of the LORD, that will I seek after; that I may dwell in the house of the LORD all the days of my life, to behold the beauty of the LORD, and to enquire in his temple" (KJV). God isn't saying, "I'll give you whatever your heart desires." God is in fact saying, "I'll give your heart what to desire. I will retrain, redial, and reconfigure your heart to where your heart's desires become My heart's desires. Your wants exclusively become My wants."

It goes back to David's prayer in Psalm 23: "The Lord is..." And because of all that He is in my life, I shall not want anything outside of His provision.

Now, before we close, let's talk about what it means for your life to fulfill His purpose. Your life is there to fulfill His dreams and His hopes for the world and for His kingdom. What if your morning prayer was "Lord, may I fulfill Your purpose today? May I fulfill Your dreams today? May I fulfill Your will today?" What if your daily surrender was because of who He is and not who you are? "Lord, I will not want anything. I will not allow my heart to desire anything outside of what You have provided. So in other words, if You ain't providing it, I ain't wanting it, Lord. One thing have I desired. And that is simply what You have for me."

God is saying, "Over time as you walk with Me and sit in My presence, I'll dial your heart back to one thing. Your desires and your longings will become like My longings. Your heart will learn and will be retrained. It will be reconfigured and daily readjusted to desire what I have for you." So, let's get our dreams out of the way so that we can spend time fulfilling His dreams for our life.

Remember, we won't be perfect. We won't get it right. That's why there's a beautiful thing called grace. We will fail miserably and make huge mistakes. We'll go on long runs of getting it right and then we'll hit a wall or a pothole, and we'll find ourselves off the wagon looking at something we shouldn't have looked at or consuming something we know isn't good for us. We won't get it right. So build in room for God's grace, because it's not about our perfection. It's about His perfection and Him perfecting all things inside of us.

One of my favorite hymns is " 'Tis So Sweet to Trust in Jesus." It tells us that it is sweet just to trust Him—just to take Him at His word, and rest upon His promise. My favorite part is the last line of the chorus that says, "Oh, for grace to trust him more."

Postlude

When I hear it and when I sing it, I hear failure baked into the phrase. It's this idea that I wanna trust You and I'll get grace to trust You more. But then I fail and oh, I'll get more grace so I can trust You more the next time. And then I'll fail. And then I'll get more grace to trust You more the next time. And yes, there is progression. There is growth. I do get better, but there is still failure. Friends, failure will be a part of our story. Sin and falling will be a part of our story, but oh for grace to trust Him more the next time. We are always praying for greater grace. A greater grace, a greater failure, a greater grace—it's a pattern. That's why it is so sweet to trust in Jesus. Even when He feels like a disobedient God, what He really is, is a God who's worthy to be trusted.

So, I pray that we would find friends who hang in the dust and push us to accountability, to hope, to purpose, and to God. And I pray that we would find rest in God's sovereignty—that we would know that at the beginning of time, He was there, and at the end of time, He will be there. So in the meantime, may we find ourselves right here in His presence. And may we rest well, knowing that we were designed with this kind of crisis of wind and storm and chaos in mind. In order to rest well, may we have a peace that passes all understanding, and Father, would You guard our hearts and our minds every step of the way. And to that end, we surrender our dreams so that we might get after Yours. May our life be used for the fulfillment of Your hopes, Your dreams, and Your purpose for the earth, and may our heart's desires be Your desires. And, finally, when failure comes and when sin gets the best of our hand, oh for grace to trust You more—may we know the sweetness of trusting You. Amen.

Acknowledgments

I want to acknowledge my amazing, intelligent, beautiful wife for always extending me so much grace and for giving me time to sit, reflect, read, write, and create content that hopefully not only blesses the world, but blesses you, too. Thank you so much for your unwavering belief in me and your support.

To my children, Zoe, Bethany, Isaac, and Micah, thank you so much for allowing Dad to take time to create this work that hopefully blesses the world, and you as well. As you go on your own faith journeys, I want you to know that when God goes off-script, you can still trust Him. Always follow Him even in His disobedience, because even there, He is faithful, He is sovereign, and He is good. Thank you for all your support and for allowing me to be who God has called me to be. And always remember, even when I am called to be a writer or preacher or pastor, my first call and priority is to be your dad—and it is my greatest joy. I love you. Thank you.

About the Author

Albert Tate is the founding and lead pastor of Fellowship Church in Los Angeles County, California. He began his ministry pastoring just a few families at Sweet Home Church in Mississippi before serving the historic Lake Avenue Church in Pasadena, California. Hearing the call from God to plant a church, Albert and his wife, LaRosa, launched Fellowship Church in January 2012. In its short history, this gospel-centered, multiethnic, intergenerational church has already established a solid foothold in the region to the glory, honor, and transformational power of Christ. As a dynamic communicator, Albert is passionate about sharing the gospel of Jesus Christ both locally and globally. He serves on the board of trustees at Azusa Pacific University; the Global Leadership Network; and Stadia,

195

a global church-planting organization. Albert is the founder and CEO of The Greatest Story, Inc., and president of Harambee Ministries. He recently published his first book, entitled *How We Love Matters: A Call to Practice Relentless Racial Reconciliation*. Albert is the proud father of four children: Zoe, Bethany, Isaac, and Micah.